Riding with the
Phoenix

TO FIND A NEW MORAL IMPERATIVE

George E. Monroe, Ph.D.

authorHOUSE®

AuthorHouse™ LLC
1663 Liberty Drive
Bloomington, IN 47403
www.authorhouse.com
Phone: 1-800-839-8640

Published by AuthorHouse 08/20/2014

ISBN: 978-1-4969-3030-9 (sc)
ISBN: 978-1-4969-3031-6 (e)

Library of Congress Control Number: 2014914916

Contents

To the Reader

The basic premise of this book was conceived more than twelve years ago. At that time, the primary intention was to share a profound revelation that came to me in flash of *awareness* as I reflected on the insights of three seminal authors. The first version was self-published in 2001. The original title was, *Mitchell's Point: Journey To Where You Can See Forever.* A revised version with the same title was self-published in 2006. Self-publishing was employed as the best means to get this critical discovery into print and test public response to it while retaining the ability to continue developing its presentation. In this way, it has been a book in progress since 2001. This is the third and much expanded version. It remains true to the original premise of sharing the revelation.

However, I continued to expand the content of the book as relevant memories and new experiences coalesced into broader perspectives. Eventually, a secondary premise came into focus. It was to illustrate how extraordinary experiences and personal decisions resulted in realizing a revelation from the Universal Mind. In processing the information that led to that premise, I also realized that it was important to illustrate and validate the extraordinary experiences and decisions of potential readers on their own unique journeys through life. Helping them to become aware of the commonalities they shared despite their differences was essential to their understanding and accepting the unique content of the book.

A third premise of the book emerged as my awareness evolved to the point where I realized I could offer vital new perspectives for human beings living in a troubled but promising time on the edge of a renaissance about to unfold.

While the content of the book is primarily based on the author's extraordinary life experiences and insights, it also is based on his observations of similar experiences and insights of other sagacious life travelers. The amalgamated narrative follows the main character on his journey through a life filled with daunting obstacles and exhilarating opportunities. It is unique to his time and circumstances but it mirrors many aspects of the journey made by each person within their own *zeitgeist*. You will be able to see how this composite retrospection validates your own unusual experiences and thoughts, many of which you may have suppressed or rejected because you thought they were too *different* to be shared.

You will follow Gregg from the time he arrives in the world, squalling, hungry, and barely conscious. You will travel with him through many personal trials and firsthand witnessing that lead him toward ever more encompassing perspectives. You will be with him when he realizes he has often accessed universal energy, symbolized by the archetypical legend of the *Phoenix,* to rise up from crushing losses and turn them into exciting new challenges. You will see that eventually he gains sufficient awareness to connect with the Universal Mind. You will witness his transcendent discovery distilled from the inspired research and insights of several other extraordinary explorers. And, you will be with him when he proposes that this divine gift from the Universal Mind can enable human beings to find the new moral imperative needed to create and manage a new golden age.

ACKNOWLEDGEMENTS

First and foremost I want to thank my wife and partner, Merle Monroe, for patiently supporting me throughout the challenging process of writing this book. Her vision that I was a capable instrument and had an important contribution to make compelled my best efforts to bring forth something illuminating and useful. She taught me (over and over again) how to use the computer, made countless corrections when I fouled up, relieved my panic by retrieving copy I somehow lost in the bowels of the hard drive, and commiserated with me when I forgot to save my work. It is doubtful that this book would have been written without her competent assistance and caring encouragement.

My debt is very large to two exceptional people, Susan Lazar and Catherine Schuler, for many hours of stimulating discussions that helped to shape the tone and content of the book, for believing in me and the importance of the book's purpose, and for many more hours they spent in careful reading and editing of pages, chapters, and several revisions of the whole manuscript.

I owe much to Norman Overly who graciously consented to apply his academic expertise and extraordinary awareness to editing the manuscript when I was much in need of a competent editorial review by someone outside of my very supportive in-group. The technical corrections and suggestions he made enabled me to change what I had written from "an interesting collection" to a unified volume.

I am deeply grateful to my teacher, friend, and mentor, Maxine Dunfee, who supported my creative efforts when I was a rough but promising talent in her undergraduate education classes. She taught me how to engage students in experiential learning, offered encouragement as my academic career unfolded, helped me make creative contributions as editor of the Newsletter of the World Council for Curriculum and Instruction (WCCI), and was a supportive contributor to this book from its initial conception to completion of the first published version.

Special recognition is due to my special friend Pamela Cramer for her enthusiastic interest in what I was writing and her thoughtful reflections about it. Besides listening patiently on several occasions while I read key chapters of the first version to her, she asked many penetrating questions that helped me clarify my thinking.

For enthusiastic response to the second published version and expert help in revising it to improve narrative flow, update the content to include more examples of transcendent experiences, design a more interesting cover, and create a new title that reflected the broadened scope of the book, I owe much to my unusually perceptive friend and professional associate, Hall Healy.

PROLOGUE

Gregg once heard a story about Albert Einstein that he called on thereafter whenever he needed to calm down. It seems that Dr. Einstein and a colleague went to a restaurant to have some lunch. They each ordered soup and a sandwich. When the young waitress realized whom she would be serving, she became very nervous. As she started to place Dr. Einstein's soup in front of him, she stubbed her toe and spilled some of the soup in his lap. She was mortified. He calmly placed a hand on her shoulder and gently asked if she could bring a wet cloth to wipe away the soup. His kindly manner reassured the girl and she hurried off to the kitchen for a cloth. When she was out of hearing range, his colleague questioned why Einstein didn't demand an apology or call the manager and have the waitress fired. He was quite surprised by the thoughtful response: "Well, when I consider that here we are on this spinning ball of rock we call the earth…and it is revolving around the sun that is actually a star… and this star revolves around the center of a group of stars we call a galaxy…and our sun is one of the smaller stars out near the edge of this rotating galaxy that contains billions of stars…and this galaxy is one of many billions of galaxies in the universe…then I think to myself, what is a little soup on somebody's pants?"

This story fit neatly with how Dr. Einstein was said to observe the world. He positioned his mind at a vantage point where he could view the earth within a very broad perspective. Many things that loomed large on the surface of the earth seemed insignificant when examined from locations that were far out in space. The celestial magnificence of this broadly inclusive view convinced him that there was a great deal more to the universe than was ordinarily visible from an earthbound position. It was where he tuned in to information within the Universal Mind and recorded what he heard when his inner mind connected with that universal source.

Dr. Edgar Mitchell was one of the Apollo Astronauts who went to the moon in 1971. That journey changed his life profoundly. Riding back toward the earth in the *Kittyhawk* command module, he observed the earth from a vantage point far out in space. In his groundbreaking book, *The Way of The Explorer,* he wrote that he "had time to relax in weightlessness and contemplate that blue jewel-like home planet suspended in the velvety blackness from which we had come." He said he felt an overwhelming sense of *connectedness.* It occurred to him that the universe was somehow conscious. That its existence, and their presence as space travelers within it, was not accidental. That there was an intelligent process at work.

Both Einstein and Mitchell had something in common that helped them expand their perspectives. They looked at the earth and human life from an extraterrestrial vantage point far out in space. Gregg had seen actual photographs of the earth taken from the window of Mitchell's spacecraft at a point shortly after departure from the moon. He felt they had a spiritual beauty that was surely the creation of a super intelligence. He examined those photographs often. Taken from a point far out in space that he respectfully referred to as *Mitchell's Point.* He found he could send his mind (perception) out there and view things from that location. Where he could feel connected to the universe. Where he could tune in to information in the energy field of the Universal Mind. Where he could understand that he was a part of the Universal Mind. Where his conscious mind would clear and his perspective on the problems of life on the earth would include visions of opportunities for creative solutions.

CHAPTER I

A Treasure Lost

Nothing has really happened until it has been recorded.

---Virginia Woolf

The past is but the past of a beginning.

---H. G. Wells

A funeral triggers painful but therapeutic retrospection

It was a very hot summer morning. The sun was already high in the sky. The grass man for Budde's Funeral Home was busy covering the freshly dug earth with worn mats of artificial grass. A canvas canopy was erected beside the open grave. Racks of flowers were set in place. Just in time. The procession of flagged funeral vehicles, led by the old Cadillac hearse, was already entering the cemetery. The roadway up from the entrance was a single trail of little used tire tracks with grass growing up the middle. At the north end of the cemetery the road turned to the right and made a great loop around the upper two-thirds of the burial plots to rejoin the single roadway that was both entrance and exit for the lower third. The hearse moved slowly up the gentle hill and around the loop. At the urging of the grass man, the procession of flagged vehicles followed in close pursuit. When the last one was in the loop, the undertaker moved the hearse back onto the single lane and down the hill a few yards to the grave site. Some of the procession was able to follow. The rest of the vehicles were inadvertently trapped on the loop. People got out and walked to where the burial ceremony would take place.

Two dozen folding chairs inside the canopy were reserved for close family members. A few others were lucky enough to find standing room under the eaves. There was no other shade anyplace nearby, so the rest had to endure the boiling sun. They hoped the minister would show mercy and be brief. With the open location of the ceremony and their vehicles locked in, there was little chance for escape. It was a country preacher's dream come true.

Gregg was already starting to sweat. He always sweated at funerals whether it was cold or hot. His undershorts were starting to get wet and pinch in unhandy places. He tried to rearrange them to a more comfortable position by quick tugs he hoped no one would notice. After a long day at the office he had taken a red-eye flight east from Seattle to attend the funeral of his beloved Uncle Ray. He didn't get much sleep on the plane. An overbearing man who had too much to drink talked incessantly to the bored woman in the seat beside him. Then the cab driver that brought him from the airport turned out to be a talker. During the hour's ride he never paused for more than 30 seconds. Gregg arrived in town just in time to walk to the cemetery. He was still in the clothes he wore to work the day before. He had washed his face and brushed his teeth in the toilet on the plane. He wished he had been able to take a shower and shave.

The Funeral Director was seating the family members. In the front row, at the edge of the burial pit, he placed Uncle Ray's wife, his daughter, two sisters, a brother and the minister. Gregg was motioned into the chair behind the wife and daughter. This made him sweat even more. He really loved his uncle. Over the years he had observed the abuse his uncle and his niece had endured at the hand of Auntie Vera. Sitting so close at the funeral of his beloved uncle stirred painful memories. "She should be in the box," he thought. "It isn't fair that she drove him to an early grave and sits here today mostly thinking about what she will inherit."

As the preacher droned on, Gregg had a difficult time staying focused on his voluminous eulogizing. His mind wandered from vengeful wishes for Auntie Vera to pleasant memories of his Uncle Ray. He especially remembered the Sunday fishing trips his uncle organized. He always included as many family members and friends as he could entice to come along. It was the good times with people that he loved. Fishing was a way to get them together. When they went fishing there was always plenty of good food with cold drinks spread out on a makeshift table beside a creek or lake. Watermelons cooled in tubs of iced water were often available under insulated wraps. They were kept "until later" in the back of his flat bed truck that also served as group transportation. Usually, someone brought a guitar and started singing around a smoky campfire in the evening. Uncle Ray loved the singing. He also loved to tell stories. He constantly gathered story material from books, magazines, his own experiences, and people he met in his travels as a long distance truck driver. He especially liked mysteries and was big fan of *Ripley's Believe It Or Not.* In the flickering light of a campfire, he would spin marvelous (and almost believable) mystery tales. He also told some fascinating stories about his experiences when he was drafted to drive trucks for the U.S. Army in the jungles of Asia. When he wasn't telling stories or eating or singing, he wandered around and visited with people; especially the kids. He was really there for the kids. He baited hooks for the little ones. He untangled their lines when they got snagged. If lines were broken he replaced the lost hooks and sinkers. He fashioned hook removers from slender willow sticks and used them to carefully extricate hooks from fish that had swallowed them. He had a special grip for handling slippery catfish with poisonous spines and powerful jaws full of pinpoint teeth. If someone had the bad luck to catch a snapping turtle or a hated waterdog, he would cut the line and take the hapless creature someplace where it wouldn't be seen again. However, as time passed Gregg began to realize that behind the atmosphere of fun and fellowship Auntie Vera was nastily berating Uncle Ray with complaints and ridicule. She hated his family and imagined (or realized) that they also hated her. Uncle Ray would enjoy moments with his relatives and friends, only to get shot down by his wife when they were out of hearing range or in the car on the way home. Gregg had trouble believing her tears now at his uncle's graveside, unless they represented the loss of a captive she could torment.

He became aware that his thoughts about Auntie Vera were making him feel sad and angry. So he tried to change the focus of his ruminating. He tried to think of things that would distract him from the droning of the preacher. He wasn't having much luck until he caught a glimpse of something on the mound of plastic grass across the burial pit. It was green and blended in, but its quick movements from spot to spot gave it away. He strained to keep it in focus and follow its activities. When it moved close enough, he could see that it was a salamander. He sat mesmerized by this tiny green survivor with an ancient ancestry. No doubt a key feature in the survival of its species was the fact that it had developed two keen and independent eyes. They could each be rotated to provide a panoramic view of the world around it. Gregg wondered what information was within the genes of this little green creature that had enabled its kind to survive and prosper when many other larger and fearsome creatures had long since gone to extinction.

Then he noticed the grass man sitting in the shadow cast by the panel truck he used to haul the plastic grass. He was waiting for the ceremony to be over so he could pack up and head back to the Funeral Home. Fascinated, Gregg suddenly remembered that he had been a grass man once, near the end of World War II. He was fifteen at the time and looked a little older. All of the able-bodied men from his hometown were either in active military service or working overtime in civilian jobs supporting the war effort. The local Funeral Director asked him if he would put out the plastic grass for a funeral and he agreed. That part of the job was easy and kind of fun. He got to drive a panel truck to and from the cemetery. The Funeral Director was an elderly man who had come back from retirement to mind the store while his son was in the army. He didn't trust his own driving. After the funeral was over, he asked Gregg to drive him to a hospital in the city. He didn't make it clear that they would be going to the morgue to pick up someone who had recently died there. They arrived at the morgue just as an autopsy on the deceased was being completed. The naked body of an emaciated old woman lay on a refrigerated stainless steel table. Big incisions across the upper chest and lower abdomen were joined by another cut straight up the middle. The result was two huge door-like flaps that were opened wide from the center to allow unrestricted examination. The examiner randomly stuffed handfuls of organs back into the body cavity, closed the flaps, and left the room. The elderly Funeral Director told Gregg to grab the cadaver by the ankles so they could load it into a body bag. He first drew back in revulsion and then did as he was told. On the trip back to Sand Point he declined an offer to stop for a bite to eat. Later he helped to unload the bag into the embalming room at the Funeral Home. He wondered if he would ever get his hands clean again. He also vowed that it was his last day on the job.

The minister's droning seemed to be slowing down a little. He was emphasizing some points with short bursts of increased volume, either to drive them home or to wake up those who had tuned out. The salamander sat atop the grass-covered mound beside the pit and surveyed the dismal scene. Its two eyes rotated constantly, like tiny radar antennas, picking up and processing information. Gregg wondered what the wily little creature was seeing and what survival strategies were being activated from its genetic archives. He wasn't sure why he had the strong intuition that its appearance there, in that unlikely time and place, was no coincidence.

A small cloud briefly blocked the sun and made it a little darker at the scene. Perhaps the minister took it as a signal to wind down his remarks. He came to a close and suggested a moment of silent prayer. Gregg mused that bowed heads and silence seemed altogether fitting to the somber surroundings in dimmed light. He noticed that Auntie Vera was fidgeting in her chair; anxious to get the deed done and move on. "Treasures are always put in boxes and then hidden away to be lost or forgotten," he thought. "Uncle Ray is a treasure. He's about to be put in a box and then a vault where he'll be hidden away. He'll be a lost treasure in due time, as memories dim and those who knew him pass from the scene."

When the prayer ended, the minister nodded to the Funeral Director who signaled the grass man to release the brake on the mechanism that held the casket over the grave. The casket was slowly lowered into the vault. Then the grass man and a helper hooked heavy canvas straps to the concrete lid and let it down carefully onto the tar-covered edges of the vault. The squished tar would form a water-tight seal. The straps were removed and placed behind the grass-covered mound. A few family members and friends came by to toss a handful of dirt on the vault. The Funeral Director got into the hearse and drove out of the cemetery. Family and friends returned to their cars and followed behind. Gregg stayed a little while to watch the grass man put the plastic grass into the panel truck and head back to the Funeral Home. When he was alone, he said a few words to his beloved Uncle Ray and then walked away as the diggers stashed the remainder of their six-pack and moved in to fill the pit.

As Gregg was walking from the cemetery into town a car pulled beside him and slowed down. He turned toward the car and a window opened. Two men were in the front seat. The one on the passenger side called his name.

"Gregg, old buddy, is that you?"

"The last time I checked it was still me. Who are you?"

"Don't you recognize your old high school buddies?"

The car stopped. Gregg stepped closer and studied the middle-aged faces without a glimmer of recognition. Then the driver spoke.

"Dammit, Gregg. Its Lonzo Hobbs and Bill Turner. We heard you were in town for your uncle's funeral. Get in and let's go over to the Corncrib where we can talk."

"Good idea. Son-of-a-bitch! I still can't believe it's you two."

He got into the back seat and they headed for the bar. The Corncrib was a short order restaurant and tavern that occupied most of the first floor of a rambling two-story wood building. The upper floor had been empty for a long time. Gregg and his old buddies slid into a booth near the back of the main room where new Model A Fords once had been displayed for sale. The walls were covered with weathered lumber supposedly salvaged from old corncribs. A hand operated corn sheller and other collectibles sat on crude shelves or hung from randomly spaced nails. A few regulars sat at the bar, nursing their beers and talking politics. The lunch crowd hadn't yet arrived. The special of the day was corn bread and beans with sliced tomatoes. Gregg ordered the king-sized beef burger with fries and a frosted mug of beer. His buddies ordered the same. When the bartender/waiter headed for the kitchen, they turned to each other. Lonzo was the first to speak.

"Dammit Gregg, I'm sure sorry about your Uncle Ray. He was one helluva guy. It seems like a hundred years ago, but I still remember the fishin' trips he dragged us on like they happened yesterday. Lots of tasty food. Campfires and singin'. Practical jokes. And his special mystery stories. Sometimes I was afraid to go off in the dark to take a piss after he told a scary one."

Bill nodded in agreement, then started to laugh as he took over. "Yeah, the mystery stories were fun. And they always made you think. But the practical jokes were really a hoot. Remember when we fooled ol' Granny Anderson into thinkin' she was the supreme expert at catchin' fish? She was always braggin' about somethin'. That time she told a whopper about all the fish she caught once and started advisin' the little kids about how to fish the right way. We cooked up a scheme to get her to set her pole and come up by the picnic table to help with the food while we hooked a dead fish on her line. She couldn't see very well and didn't realize the fish was dead. Every time she went back to her pole there was another fish on the line. Being good and helpful boys, we volunteered to take the fish off her hook and put them on a stringer. Every time she (caught) another fish, she bragged about her foolproof method. She must've (caught)

7

forty fish that day. She told the little kids that they should just set their poles and go away a little while and then come back and there would be a fish on the line. She was all puffed up proud and we were laffin' our asses off."

Bill broke in, "yeah, the stringer *somehow* got untied and all the fish got away. She was so pissed and never did know the difference."

Lonzo took back the lead. "Man, the most fun was when Orville was drivin' the truck back home in the dark after a fishin' trip. There was a bunch of people in the back and they were singin' and laughin' and havin' a jolly old time. Orville knew where someone had run over a big animal, a dog or 'coon or something, and it had been layin' out in the sun all day and got really ripe. When he spotted that carcass layin' in the road up ahead, he reached down and pulled out the choke on that old truck so the engine started coughin' and spittin' and slowin' down. Orville eased the truck to a stop right over that putrid carcass and rolled up the windows on the cab. Right away people in the back started groanin' and coughin' and holdin' their noses. Orville *tried* to start the truck and got it to move forward just past the carcass. Someone in the back grabbed a flashlight and shined it on the road. Next thing you heard was people screamin' and pukin' and cussin' ol' Orville. He was in the cab laffin' his ass off. Me and Bill and some of the other boys jumped out and ran down the road 'til we was out of smellin' range. Then Uncle Ray came along and blasted his horn at Orville which broke up the party. Orville drove ahead slowly and stopped up the road to let everybody get back on the truck. Later, Uncle Ray gave ol' Orville hell but he could hardly keep from laffin' when he did it."

Gregg raised his hand to indicate he had a good one to share. "This one's about high school. When ol' Virgil Bunker finally got his. He was always doin' something sneaky and then braggin' about how he got away with it. He would strut around all cocky-like and piss everybody off. He found a way to be the first one outside the building when the last bell rung at the end of the day, by sneakin' in the fire escape chute and slidin' down to the ground outside. When the rest of us came out the front door he was already on his bike and sayin' smart-alecky things just to aggravate everybody. Then ol' Max Henderson figured out how to settle him down. In the middle of the afternoon he got excused. Instead of goin' to the boy's toilet in the basement, he went outside and crawled quietly up the fire escape chute and took a crap just outside the chute door on the second floor. Virgil's system was to get one of the girls to go up to talk to the study hall teacher just about time for the bell to ring. When the teacher was distracted, ol' Virgil would quickly open the fire escape door and launch hisself down the chute. That time you could hear ol' Virgil yell '**shiiit**' all the way down. We all hurried outside but ol' Virgil wasn't anywhere around. He had gone straight to the woodshed back of his house. The incident was investigated the next day. Nobody knew anything and Virgil didn't dare tell, so the principal made ol' Virgil go up in the chute and wash it down."

The three men exchanged story after story. Each remembrance triggered up another. They laughed and laughed. Tears rolled down their cheeks. They lost count of how many times the bartender refilled their mugs with cold beer. Time passed without notice. Eventually, the focus returned to memories of Uncle Ray. How he helped the little kids with their fishing problems. How he got everybody to sing and love it. How he was always good for a small loan if you were running a little short. How everybody always paid him back because it was Uncle Ray and they didn't want to disappoint him. How he took so much crap from Auntie Vera and never let it get him down or change him. And how he told his really special stories in the dark by the dying campfires just before time to pack up and go home. They retold a few of their favorites. There was one mystery story he told about lost treasure that made everybody want to look for it. He made it sound like it was more valuable than any treasure they had ever heard of before and he said they could find it if they tried hard enough. It always seemed as if it was not far away. Gregg remembered that when they had begged for more clues Uncle Ray told them to think about it often and one day, when they were ready, they would find all the clues they needed. Gregg's mind flashed back to the salamander he saw earlier in the day. For a fleeting instant he had a very strange thought. He wondered if the appearance of the little green creature at Uncle Ray's funeral was somehow related to the mysterious treasure he had occasion to "think about often" over the years.

CHAPTER II

Stranger In Paradox

One who gains strength by overcoming obstacles possesses
the only strength that can overcome adversity.

---Albert Schweitzer

Finding that he didn't fit where Providence had placed him

Gregg was sitting in the Indianapolis Airport, waiting for his flight
back to Seattle. His mind was churning with thoughts of his uncle's
funeral and the reverie with his old high school buddies. He tried to
shake his mild depression by reading a magazine. It didn't work. His
mind went racing back to his hometown. The place where he was a
puzzle piece that didn't fit. Where he grew up like a lone thistle in a
patch of clover. In a primitive cradle where he was rocked to extreme
alertness for personal survival. Certainly not the comforting peace of
inclusion based on conformity. So many images. Some very familiar.
Some long forgotten, now churning up to the conscious level. Lots of
them funny enough to evoke involuntary laughter. Many nightmarish
scenes, abusive and very painful. Recollections of a few people who
quietly nurtured and supported him when most of the community
was putting him down. At the time, he was grateful for their help.
They always seemed to appear and assist him just when he felt like
he was "going down for the count." Now, in retrospect, he realized
these rescues were not coincidental. They were a crucial part of his

11

life journey. They allowed him to stay alive as an *outsider* where he could be free to learn bigger truths.

For the little town of Sand Creek, he was an enigma from the beginning. He arrived when he was two years old because his parents had divorced. His mother had contracted tuberculosis and needed medical treatment her ne'er-do-well husband could not afford. Her mother and father had agreed to have her and the two grandchildren move in with them until she was well again. Gregg was more fair skinned and blond than his peers. He had a bigger head than most and a cowlick like Alfalfa of *The Little Rascals.* He had spontaneously learned to read and spell by the time he was four years old. For lack of any other resources, he was placed in the first grade at the local Public School the day after his fifth birthday.

His mother's tuberculosis was rendered inactive for a time. She eventually returned to high school and graduated as Gregg finished eighth grade. Then she started college. The strain of trying to care for two children, living in her parents' household, commuting forty miles each day, and competing with much better prepared students, soon took its toll. Her tuberculosis came out of hiding and she spent the next four years in a sanatorium high on a bluff overlooking the Ohio River at the bottom of the state. The treatments for her disease at that time were draconian. She had many serious operations. All of her ribs on the left side were eventually removed and her left lung was collapsed. These years were also war years. Gasoline and tires were severely rationed. Visits from her family were necessarily few and far between. Gregg rarely saw her. Despite her illness, he felt she had abandoned him.

Life in the schools of Sand Creek was a mixed bag for Gregg. There were the challenges and rewards of learning. More often there were punishments and ridicule by both teachers and peers. He quickly got bored and created diversions for his amusement. If teachers misunderstood something, or got an explanation mixed up, Gregg didn't hesitate to set them straight. It was rare that he was given credit for his insights. Most of his teachers regarded him as a nuisance to be tolerated. A first grade teacher once humiliated him and locked him in a closet because he was "too enthusiastic." A fifth grade teacher with a reputation for iron handed discipline paddled him numerous times while making him bend over a desk in front of the class. More than one gym teacher dealt with his difference by putting him in football games or boxing matches where others were slyly encouraged to give him some bruises or a bloody nose. Despite the fact that he was two or three years younger, and therefore smaller than most of them, he was shamed and called a sissy if he complained. Under such circumstances, he developed survival strategies that kept him from serious harm most of the time. He stayed near protective adults. He made a sport of avoiding bullies. He devised secret pathways for getting wherever he needed to go. He randomly executed quick changes of direction. And he practiced high speed running as a way to escape surprise confrontations. If he outsmarted his tormentors, it only made them more determined to get him. When he felt the odds for escape were in his favor, he often made it even more interesting by taunting them from a distance or out of a window. Sometimes he miscalculated, or was just unlucky, and unwittingly fell into their hands.

One such occasion nearly resulted in his demise. He was captured while swimming at the old swimming hole in Salt Creek. Two bigger boys held him by the ankles and lowered him from the end of the diving board until his eyes were under water. For what seemed like hour, they threatened to lower him further until water ran into his nose. Finally, they made good on their threats and held him there "long enough to teach him a lesson." Within a few seconds Marvin Dobbs, who had been plowing in a nearby field, stepped through the tall horseweeds and asked what was happening. Startled by his appearance, they let go and Gregg slipped totally under water. His captors didn't know that he could hold his breath long enough to swim the entire length of the swimming pool at the nearby state park. Once underwater, he realized he could use that ability to put these boys on the spot and win his release. He went limp and stayed down until he could feel them grab his arms and drag him out of the water. They laid him on the diving board and tried to drain the water they felt must be in his lungs. He stayed limp until he heard Marvin say, "You assholes have drowned him. That's first degree murder." When Gregg slowly seemed to come around and opened his eyes, they were extremely relieved to be off the hook for causing his death. They stood him on his feet and started cussing him. They told him the whole thing was his fault for being so dammed smartass. Then they kicked him from behind several times and told him to go home and keep his mouth shut about what had happened. But when he was a few yards away, Gregg turned and yelled out the most defiant response he could think of, "Marvin was right, you are assholes." And he then flew up the road to the safety of his grandparents' house. As he revisited the near disaster and the horror of this experience, Gregg wondered if Marvin's appearance at that critical time was just lucky or another one of those events in his life that was no coincidence.

He almost missed the announcement that his plane was ready for boarding because he was so deeply involved in his memories. He caught the last call and scrambled for the gate, arriving just as they were ready to close the door. He breathlessly took his seat in a three-seat row. The passenger in the aisle seat was soon sleeping quietly. The middle seat was unoccupied. He was grateful for the extra space and glad to be alone with his thoughts. As he refocused on his life as a boy in Sand Creek, many other painful thoughts came roiling up. How three of his aunts paid his way to Hilltop Camp one summer, where he was so animated in tap dancing class that he bloodied his nose with his own knee and was severely scolded for being rowdy. How in sixth grade the teacher had a fit when the state administered achievement test scores were delivered and his was the second highest in the class. How the teacher sarcastically mocked him and told the class that his high score was not deserved because he didn't study. How at the end of eighth grade, a group of kids surrounded him outside of the drugstore and humiliated him by pouring green paint all over him for "his initiation as a freshman."

How he was two or three years younger than his classmates and still riding a bicycle when they were driving cars and going on dates. How bullies were encouraged to jump out of hiding and hit him with their fists before he knew what was coming. How bigger boys would grab him and perform a painful "dutch rub" of his standout white hair while holding him firmly in a suffocating headlock. How he took a lot of dares and did crazy stuff to demonstrate his skills and try to get along. Nobody ever jumped a bicycle as fast and as high as he did. He could close his eyes now and see the big gravel pile in the vacant lot at the bottom of the steep hill on the old north road into town. He would come down the hill at very high speed and steer right at the gravel pile, sailing up and over it to unbelievable heights before landing upright on the other side. Just like Evel Knievel. When the word was out that he would be jumping, a crowd would usually gather. Bets were placed on whether he would make it. Those who were betting that he wouldn't make it tried to spook him into cracking up. He always disappointed them. None of them had the guts to try it themselves which made his triumphs all the sweeter. It was clear that he was different. The way his difference was treated made him use his ingenuity to compensate. However, many of the things he did to compensate only magnified the difference and made him more of a target for the regulars.

Other compensating activities were private. Gregg liked to sing and for a time he enjoyed the special recognition he got from exercising his choirboy voice. As taunts of his peers and even some adults grew stronger, he increasingly declined to sing in public. He sang only when he was alone. His favorite singing place was in the woods. He would find a small tree on a hill overlooking the town and climb to a comfortable perch near the top. There he would sway and sing for hours at a time, all by himself.

Becoming aware of cracks in the prevailing wisdom

Many of his behaviors seemed erratic but were purposefully done *instead of* what was considered normal in Sand Creek. They supported his feelings of being an *outsider* and sharpened his skills at survival. He learned to pay attention to what he saw. He became acutely aware of cracks in the prevailing wisdom. He was forced to rely on his own intuitions and judgments. He grew to have increasing faith in himself in spite of the fact the most of the folks he lived with repeatedly let him know he was wrong. Under these circumstances, Gregg's life in Sand Creek was often painful and always paradoxical. Yet, there came a time when he was profoundly grateful for the gift of that paradox. What made him an outsider there kept him from being accepted and therefore he was not programmed into the local culture with all of its blind spots and limitations.

Two confrontations with local religion stood out as primary factors in Gregg's early disenchantment with local religious practice. The first one occurred when he was about nine years old. He was walking along a country road when a car approached and stopped to offer him a lift. The driver soon began to talk about religion. He said that Gregg should join his church because only members of that church would be going to heaven. Then he added what he must have thought would cause enough fear to gain Gregg's compliance, "Everyone else is going to hell."

"What about people who never heard of your church?"

"They'll be damned and go to hell."

"Do you really think that God is that mean, that he would send people to hell that never heard of that rule?"

The Driver grew beet red and exploded at Gregg. He skidded the car to a stop in the middle of the gravel road.

"Get out you little bastard. The Devil has already got you."

Gregg did as he was told and the driver raced away in a great cloud of dust. He watched the car disappear around a curve and thought to himself, "That was fun."

The second religious confrontation occurred when he was ten or eleven and invited a boy from the wrong side of town to go with him to church. The minister had been "evangelizing" folks to join the church for two or three weeks. The boy Gregg invited took a bath and put on clean clothes. Though his sweater was clean, it had a rip at the elbow of the left sleeve. Upon entering the church they were quickly spotted by the minister's wife who motioned for them to join her in the vestibule. When they got there she said to follow her out to the parking lot. She took Gregg aside and told him that his companion was not suitably dressed for church because his sweater was ripped. Gregg protested that since the boy and his clothes were clean the tear shouldn't matter. The discriminating rebuke was swift and clear. "He doesn't belong here." Those experiences started him on a life-long quest to find the truth about God and religion. They didn't cause him to reject religious thought, just the fallible ideas of human beings about such matters. In retrospect, he came to realize that his religious experiences in Sand Creek were paradoxically positive because they gave him the freedom to question and explore.

There were several reasons Gregg had rejected depictions of God that were promoted in the Christian churches he attended in his youth. The interpretations of bible stories by his Sunday School teachers were very often violent and negative. The fire and brimstone sermons delivered by the ministers presented God as a great protector when people followed his dictates and a wrathful Ruler who punished them severely when they did not. God was assigned attributes of jealousy, favoritism, and discrimination that reflected more of human weakness than irrefutable knowledge of the creator. There were threats that if you didn't accept all of this on faith you would surely be dammed and go to hell. Eventually, he learned that there were many more people in the world with positive views of God than there were Christians of any persuasion. With this discovery he was convinced that the concept he had been taught was based more in superstition and personal fears than anything approaching God's true nature.

Gregg felt certain that God would not have approved of much that was being promoted in his name by exclusive and excluding true believers. For a long time he managed this discrepancy between dogma and reason by taking an agnostic position. He didn't know the complete truth and he didn't know anyone who did. He did know there was something creative that was greater than himself and the world he lived in. As he came into contact with others who held similar views and read what such thinkers had written, he discovered a number of definitions which portrayed God as the source of creation, indefinable in human terms, beyond the limits of human understanding, and manifested in the world as love rather than jealous wrath and punishment.

He also discovered that such views of God had been around for a very long time. The pre-Christian Jewish Kabala had defined God as the ALL, an inclusive and compassionate view, long before such sanctified thinking was suppressed by proprietary temple elders and Roman conquerors. Buddha's preaching was indifferent to traditional gods as the means for obtaining salvation. He focused instead on compassion, liberality, truth, nonviolence, and love as pathways that could lead to ultimate (universal) truth. Edgar Cayce spoke of Universality of the Creator expressed as a loving force in the world that he intuitively described as Universal Christ Consciousness. Ralph Waldo Emerson wrote about a loving God in universal terms and preached about this view as a Unitarian minister. Dr. Emerson also believed that the universal tenets of Unitarianism made it the most appropriate religious orientation for a democratic (pluralistic) society. It was comforting to know that, despite some oppressive racial behavior as a plantation owner, Thomas Jefferson eventually moved to bring his actions in line with his Unitarian beliefs. Gregg found these views much more compatible with his intuitions than the negative and limiting myths of his fundamental Christian upbringing. He eventually joined a Unitarian Church, served on its Board of Religious Education, and helped to develop a church school program in which all of the great religions were explored. The goal was to prepare for personal choice of religious orientation at age twenty-one. At some point in his developmental journey he came in contact with a view of God as the Super Intelligence or Mind that created the Universe. He soon found himself referring to God as the Universal Mind that is everywhere, includes everything, and is manifest in everyone.

Inexplicable experiences he couldn't share with others

Some unusual things happened to Gregg during his years in Sand Creek that had the potential to get him into trouble. That potential wasn't realized because he kept them private. At the time even he thought they were too "spooky" to share with folks who would only see more reasons to put him down. When he was about eight years old he had what might now be called a near-death experience. He had his tonsils removed by a sadistic doctor who disliked children. After Gregg's mother left him with this doctor his apprehension was rewarded with sarcasm and cursing. With the help of a burly nurse, the doctor wrestled Gregg to the operating table and forced an ether mask over his face. The ether was very caustic and suffocating. He went out screaming and struggling for all he was worth. Afterward, he didn't heal very well. He bled a lot more than expected and required a big shot of Vitamin K to make his blood coagulate better. The experience left him in a state of extreme stress for several months. He felt like he had drowned and was observing his surroundings from a detached viewpoint. Rough motions or noises in a crowd made him feel like he was back in the doctor's hands and being brutally forced under the ether again. It took more than a year for him to get his balance back. Even then he would have periodic lapses into a state of being where things seemed fuzzy and not quite real. Through it all, he was painfully aware that such treatment was dreadfully wrong.

Gregg had two more near-death experiences. The next one occurred when he was about twelve years old. He was riding a borrowed bicycle without working brakes. The owner had shown him how to slow down by putting his foot on the front tire. Gregg was coming down a long steep hill on the north side of town. When he applied his foot to the front tire, it was dragged into the fork and completely locked the wheel. He was quickly thrown over the handlebars and headfirst onto the pavement. A motorist found him unconscious in a pool of blood and drove him to a local doctor's office. His mother was called and when she entered the office Gregg was lying motionless on the padded exam table. From a place above and beyond the dreadful scene, he was aware of the doctor telling her that it looked hopeless. "I don't think he is going to make it," the doctor said. Somehow, at hearing this somber news Gregg decided to come back. As his mother and the doctor started to leave the room he startled them by speaking. He was then bandaged up and sent home. Again, he felt he was witnessing it all from a place outside of himself. He was there and yet he wasn't.

The third and last near-death experience was when he had his spleen removed at age twenty-nine. A number of high stress events had severely worn him down. Then his spleen went out of control. Instead of breaking down and recycling only worn out red blood cells, it voraciously took on any red cell that came its way. Soon he was soon dangerously short of red blood cells. A diagnosis of his bone marrow where new red cells were produced showed that "production activity is at a rate normally found in cases of severe blood loss, as in a major accident." He was very sick. Also, he was very scared. Some of his diagnostic procedures were extremely painful. He felt certain his situation was hopeless. He was truly convinced he would die in surgery. He reconciled to that understanding. He wrote farewell notes and helpful instructions to people he cared about and left them in the drawer of his bedside table. And then he moved to the certainty of his death. When it didn't happen that way and he woke up to find he was still alive, he was very angry. "Dammit to hell," he thought to himself. "I did such a good job of dying and now I'm going to have to do it all over again someday." There wasn't much information available about such experiences at the time, so he didn't have any guidelines for exploring what had happened to him. However, he was left with the profound understanding that *love* mattered above all else. His roommate and the attending nurses treated him as if he deserved special attention. His life and relationship to the world took on a new meaning. And he was amazed as he experienced fleeting moments where he felt he was in harmony with a loving Universe.

Finding supportive friendship with other outsiders

During his junior year of high school Gregg had an experience that was really spooky. Because most of the able bodied men were in uniform and away from home, teenage boys in Sand Creek got lots of opportunities to be helpful to the women left behind. In some cases this led to illicit comforting, but most often it involved innocent things. Running errands. Lifting heavy objects. Chopping firewood. Making household repairs. Listening to expressions of pain. Sometimes these substitute relationships became very intense. The needs of both people and the unusual opportunities for closeness greatly magnified their feelings for each other. Gregg had this kind of relationship with a young female teacher at the high school. She was new in town and formed her attachments there without the prejudice of local history. Under the circumstances she and Gregg were both *outsiders.* Their reasons for being so were quite different but the commonalities in their lives at that time made it easy to relate. They sensed each other's needs and responded with genuine caring. Gregg looked after her with a passion. She liked his attention. She accepted him as a friend and tried to be one in return. As time passed she became aware that beneath his misfit persona there was a person of integrity and high intelligence. She talked with him about important personal things. He felt validated by her trust. While basking in the supportive cocoon of this relationship Gregg had a profound *knowing* experience. His teacher friend's husband was in the army

21

and stationed somewhere in Alabama. She asked Gregg if he would take her to the train station in Rockton on Friday evening and come back for her on Monday afternoon. He was glad to be of service and quickly agreed. He drove her to the station in Rockton shortly after school on Friday. He was with her when she purchased her round trip ticket. He wrote down her Monday arrival time. He carried her luggage on board and stowed it above her seat. He confirmed her return time and promised he'd be there to pick her up. He got off the train and waved goodbye as it pulled out of the station. However, on Monday morning he awakened early *knowing* that something had happened to change her itinerary. It was clear that she would not be returning to Rockton as scheduled. Instead she would be rerouted to the station at Milltown that was fifty miles east of Rockton. Gregg tried to put these thoughts out of his mind. He said to himself, "This is stupid. If I go to Milltown she'll be stranded in Rockton and think I'm a nut case." But the disturbing thoughts wouldn't go away. In fact, they grew stronger with every passing minute. He started toward Rockton and after about a mile he turned around and drove to Milltown. He waited nervously for the train to come in, certain he was right and afraid he was wrong. When the train stopped she stepped off, just as he knew she would. They were both amazed and felt something very special had happened.

Even with this compassionate teacher as his special friend, the stress of his *outsider* life in Sand Creek steadily loaded him down. During his junior year, he completely lost interest in the monotonous and irrelevant course work at the high school. He spent more and more time finding creative ways to be a clown and aggravate his teachers. He even antagonized those that tried to understand and work with him, including his special friend. He loved Lorna dearly and prized her friendship more than anyone could imagine. Yet, he sometimes got so unruly in her typing class that she had to send him out of the room. And he was frequently sent out of other classrooms because his actions were disturbing. He occupied the disciplinary chair in the principal's office so often that his presence there seemed to be permanent. Many of his teachers at that time were kind and reasonable people with little training in their subject matter fields or how to deal with problematic students. They were wartime pinch hitters that were substituting for regular teachers who had been drafted or volunteered to serve in the military services. Compared to the lack of interesting activity in Sand Creek, military service seemed exciting and glamorous. Gregg thought about that a lot. At the age of fifteen, it was still out of his reach.

Gregg's life that year went steadily downhill on its way to disaster. There was a temporary change for the better when Arnie came to town. Arnie was the son of the school's eccentric band director who also tried to teach general science. He wasn't prepared for the latter but since all of the qualified science teachers had been drafted, he agreed to follow the textbook and do his best. His classes were often taken up with personal stories about himself and his views of the right way to do things. He was very fastidious about cleanliness and his clothing. He let it be known that he washed his feet and changed his socks three times every day. The students mockingly gave him the nickname of *Boogus.* It was used whenever they talked about him out of his hearing range. Until Arnie arrived in Sand Creek, no one knew that *Boogus* had a son. He had been placed in a private school when his mother died a few years earlier. *Boogus* had recently remarried and then decided to bring Arnie back home to finish high school. Arnie had started his junior year at the private school. Needless to say, his studies were far ahead of what was offered in Sand Creek. Under the circumstances, he found time to coast a lot. Arnie was almost six feet tall and very handsome. Girls fantasized about him, yet avoided any serious contact. There was the problem of *Boogus* being his dad, which was bad enough. Then there was his mother's untimely death and the separation of several years in private school. Being suddenly transferred into a new school where he knew no one except his dad, it was easy to understand why he was moody and withdrawn. It didn't take long for Gregg and Arnie to find each other.

Two *outsiders* who could find comforting parallels in what life was handing them.

Arnie soon noticed Gregg's special relationship with his teacher friend. He wanted to know all about it. Gregg told Lorna about Arnie. She was distressed by the circumstances of his life and expressed sincere interest in helping him get along at the school. Before long, Gregg, Arnie, and Lorna developed a strong and supportive three-way friendship. They talked about many personal things. They became very close. Their sharing sessions grew more involved. She eventually confided that she had married her husband to get away from home. Her dad was a powerful man who ruled over his home and family without question. He had supported her going to college to be a teacher. When she was about to graduate, he told her she would be coming back home to live until she got married. While living in a dorm at the university, she had been dating a nice young man. When he indicated that he would like to marry her, she quickly accepted. She said she did it mostly to escape having to go back to the restrictive atmosphere of her father's house. A few days after they were married her husband got his draft notice. Two weeks later, he was in the army and sent to a training camp in Alabama. She took the teaching job in Sand Creek to be far away from the home she had escaped. She said that when she had gone to spend a weekend with him near his army base, she realized she didn't really love him. She knew then she had made a terrible mistake. As the year went on, she felt more and more lonely and depressed. Gregg and Arnie tried to keep her spirits up. Their talks and hand-holdings grew ever more involved. Some precious moments of intimate connection were gained by driving to movies in Rockton and sitting close in the darkened theaters.

One time, when she was going back home to spend a weekend with her family, Gregg "borrowed" his grandmother's car so he and Arnie could take her there. She took the bus to Rockton and they met her at the train station. They talked and laughed while they rode along for a couple of hours. Noticing that they were near her home and not wanting to end their fun, they decided to park awhile. She guided them to a lane that once led to a farmhouse. The house had burned and was not rebuilt on that site. She said that dating couples often parked there to have a little privacy for their amorous activities. The lane was empty. There were no other cars in sight. It was a beautiful night, and a full moon brightly lit the pleasant countryside. They sat close together and talked about their interests and concerns, including how the terrible war was intruding on their lives. She revisited how the war had given her an acceptable way to escape a restrictive home situation and, at the same time, allow her to make a serious mistake with her marriage. They got so involved in their commiserating that they lost track of the time.

When the moon suddenly went behind a cloud, Lorna became aware of how late it was and said she needed to go right away. Arnie started the car and drove several miles before she realized they had missed a turn and were going in the wrong direction. He slowed the car down and pulled onto the shoulder to make a u-turn. The shoulder was soggy from a recent rain and the wheels sank down to the axles. They were seriously stuck and it was after midnight. They noticed a farmhouse a hundred yards or so up the road. Gregg said it was likely the resident farmer would be there and could be roused to help them. Lorna agreed that there would be somebody home. She knew the farmer who lived there. She also said he knew her dad and surely would recognize her. That problem was resolved by having her lie down across the floor in the back of the car. Gregg and Arnie covered her with an old blanket they found in the trunk and topped it with their coats. Then they went to see if they could convince the farmer to bring his tractor and pull the car out of the mud. To their amazement, he was very friendly and agreed to give them a hand. When the car was back out on the pavement, they tried to pay him for his help. He said he wouldn't take anything, wished them good luck, and then went back home to resume his sleep. They were happy to be back on the road and able to get her to her parents' house before anyone there was unduly alarmed. At the same time, they felt badly about deceiving the kindly farmer who came to their rescue.

When Lorna came back to school on Monday, she told them she was badly shaken by their close call. She said that she wanted them to stop seeing each other outside of school for a while. A month went by with only warm smiles as they passed in the hallways or saw each other at basketball games and other school events. Now and then they came in brief contact at the drugstore or the only good restaurant in Sand Creek. They exchanged greetings, made a few normal social remarks, and moved on.

One afternoon Lorna told Gregg to come to her classroom at the end of the school day. When he got there she told him that she would be going to Indianapolis for a meeting of the State Teachers Association the following week. She said it would be possible to get together with him and Arnie, if they were able to join her there after the meetings were finished. He was ecstatic. They settled on a place to meet and he went to tell Arnie. On the designated day, the two of them took a bus to Indianapolis and only had to wait an hour before she appeared. She looked like Gregg's fondest vision. They hugged each other warmly and started walking toward the famous Circle Monument at the city center. There was no plan beyond just being together. They wandered in and out of stores, chattering and laughing. They went to the top of the Circle Monument and looked out over the city. They got some food and watched people go by the front window of the restaurant. Lots of military personnel were on liberty. Some with visiting family members. Some with girlfriends from home. Some with girls they met in local bars or on the street. Lots of people trying to forget about the war for a few hours and have a good time. The three friends (Gregg, Lorna, and Arnie) amused themselves by making comments on the passing scene. Then they decided to go to a movie.

The movie program was longer than expected. There were long newsreels that painted a bleak picture of how the war was going. These were followed by several previews of coming attractions. Most of them were hastily made war pictures that portrayed the allies as valiant warriors with God on their side. Then came the main feature that was mostly tolerated as a cover for the closeness that was their real focus. When they got outside afterward it was almost eleven. Time to get on a bus and go home. They walked over to the bus station and checked the schedule for the next trip to Sand Creek. They were shocked to find there was nothing going out until 8:20 the next morning! The regular trips had been cancelled because there was imminent need to make repairs on the much worn vehicle serving for a bus. Panic set in! What to do? They finally figured that there was no choice but to stay overnight in a hotel. Because it was wartime and the city was loaded with servicemen on liberty, every hotel in the immediate vicinity was fully booked. Call after call yielded the same "no vacancy" response. When they were about to give up, Gregg made one more call and got the promise of a room if he would come over right away. They had to walk about a dozen blocks to find the hotel in a rather seedy neighborhood. A room was a room, and beggars couldn't be choosers. Gregg and Arnie registered with the clerk while Lorna waited in a restaurant down the street. They checked out the room and located a stairway where the three of them could go up later without being noticed. By midnight, the unholy trio was snuggled into bed. Three extremely tired and emotionally distressed people. They were amazed at how they got there and hoped it would never end. It ended all too soon, of course, and shortly after a somber breakfast at a local café they were all on busses out of the city. Gregg and Arnie said tearful goodbyes to Lorna first. She had decided to go to Rockton and then take the shuttle bus over to Sand Creek. Gregg and Arnie went directly to Sand Creek and were waiting at the bus stop when she arrived. They helped her get her suitcase and packages over to the room she rented on the second floor of Marshall's boarding house. All three of them were keenly aware that they had experienced something wonderful but it couldn't be shared with others. They also knew it was imperative to slow the pace of their connecting while it was still private and under their control. If it got out, the community of Sand Creek would be swift to condemn their surreptitious actions. They vowed to give other interests the primary focus of their attention in the meantime.

Boredom and creativity provide a crucible for serious trouble

One day Gregg and his friend Max made a wonderful discovery. They were nosing around in the alley behind a building that had once been the site of a thriving general store. The store had gone out of business several years earlier and the building stayed empty for a long time. During WWII, a field unit of the army temporarily moved into an old Civilian Conservation Corps (CCC) Camp in the nearby state park. While this military unit was in residence, the store was converted to a makeshift USO for the soldiers who came into Sand Creek on liberty. When they moved out of the camp, the store was closed again except for a small lean-to attached to the north side of the building. It had once been used for a short-order restaurant. After the soldiers were gone, the Town Marshall rented that part of the building to house his shoe repair business. However, due to the creative efforts of Gregg and his friend Max the Marshall became the unwitting supporter of an illicit gambling den right under his little shop.

As the two boys passed the rear of the building, they noticed that some of the latticework that enclosed the underside of the back porch had rotted and fallen apart. A few gentle tugs revealed a web-covered door under the high porch that apparently led into a basement. A few more tugs and they were under the porch, breathing hard as they approached that old door. It obviously hadn't been opened for many years. They tried to push the door open. It didn't budge. Max said, "We're going to need some tools for this job. Let's close everything up and go get some." An hour later, they were back at the door with some old keys and two wrecking bars. Max said, "Let's try the keys first. If that doesn't work, we'll give it the treatment with our wrecking bars." The very first key easily turned the simple old cast-iron lock and the door swung open. They entered cautiously. When their eyes got used to the dim light, they could see that they were in a huge basement room that had once been used for storing grocery supplies. There were some old tables and chairs that probably had been moved downstairs and forgotten when the building was used for the USO. Then Max reached for one of the light sockets hanging from the ceiling and gave the switch a turn. To their great surprise, the dusty old light bulb glowed brightly. There was still electricity flowing in those old wires! What a find. A large hidden room. Right in the middle of town. Complete with furniture and electricity. It was the perfect place to do a little card playing where none of the pesky elders would be able to find them. They closed up again and went back home for "cleaning stuff" to get the place in order.

Two days later, they were ready to operate. The word spread quickly and business was brisk. Gregg and Max collected five percent of each betting pot as their fee for providing the excellent facilities, until some bigger boys objected and stopped the practice. Then some adult men figured out what was happening and came in to join the games. Gregg and Max adapted to catering refreshments and were allowed to make a small profit on the orders they went out for. The illicit enterprise they started was humming along. It was so successful that the townspeople began to notice that the streets were empty. The grocery store and restaurant owners began to comment suspiciously on the big increase in take out orders. They mentioned their observations to the Marshall and he said he would look into the situation. He nailed one younger boy on a carry out errand and demanded an explanation. Another errand boy saw the Marshall questioning his friend and alerted the card players who quickly turned out the lights and scattered. When the Marshall and his informer got there, the place was dark and empty. He didn't catch anyone else but he got enough information from the boy he had captured that he knew who was responsible. When he realized that he had been paying the electric bill for their illegal activities, he was absolutely furious. He vowed that justice would be done! In a wild- eyed rage he told his story to the County Prosecutor, a crusty old gentleman who hated kids and was always threatening to send some off to the state reform school. The Prosecutor's predicted response was a stern order to round up the boys and bring them in right away.

The angry Marshall took Gregg to the Prosecutor's office for a very threatening session. Afterward, he told Gregg that he would be watching his every move and before long he would get him put in jail. That experience caused his depression to return with a vengeance. Even so, he had to laugh when he thought of the fun they had at the Town Marshall's expense. Looking back many years later, he understood why it had been so hilarious to put one over on this man. He could have been the model for the Barney Fife character who was Andy Griffith's deputy in the mythical town of Mayberry, USA. When he went square dancing at the old country lodge on Saturday nights, his ungainly appearance also made him resemble the itinerant schoolmaster, Ichabod Crane, described in Washington Irving's *Sleepy Hollow.* And he was always threatening kids with his power as an officer of the law. Just to observe him "on duty" around the town or trying to impress the ladies with his unwitting imitations of a scarecrow on the dance floor gave numerous opportunities for hidden laughter. Many of these events also provided an endless supply of material for raunchy jokes that embellished the caricature of Sand Creek's illustrious "defender of truth, justice, and the American Way."

Too many blows and cuts started to wear him down

Three more devastating events occurred in Gregg's life during that year. Any one of them should have been enough to account for his growing depression. His aunt Lana died a horrible death from a misdiagnosed case of strep throat. The house where he had lived with his grandparents since he was two years old burned to the ground. His much beloved grandfather contracted tuberculosis and resisted leaving his family for treatment in the state sanatorium many miles away. He knew it would be difficult for his family to visit him because gasoline for civilian use was tightly rationed. He chose to stay home and slowly coughed his life away in a hospital bed set up in the house they rented after the fire. With his mother in a sanatorium and his grandmother in extreme emotional pain from her own losses, there wasn't much of a family support system for Gregg. He spent a lot of time away from home, staying with the few friends he had, until his welcome wore thin. When he did stay at home, he was often in serious conflict with his overwhelmed and distraught grandmother. The only thing that kept him from "going under" was the relationship he had with his special teacher friend. When he wasn't with her he was *dreaming* about being with her. His dreams about her were beautiful and pleasant. Certainly, the dreams continued even when he was with her. In large measure those dreams made up for the pain of his realities. He felt validated by her attention. In spite of her own pain and confusion, she wanted to give him that. They loved each other from deeper sources than either of them really understood at the time. It was partly based on compassionate response to the need they could see in each other's eyes. It was partly recognition of something attractive about their fundamental similarities. It was partly addiction to the temporary comfort they anticipated, and sometimes achieved, in contact with each other.

Then something happened that put a painful end to the cozy relationship he and Arnie enjoyed with Lorna. It seemed fine at first. Both of them thought it might provide a pleasant distraction that would reduce her marital distress. It started when a good looking young man, who was gaining prominence as a radio announcer, was transferred to a station in South Bend. He had grown up in Sand Creek and his parents still lived there. When he came into town for a visit, he happened to see Lorna walking down the street. He liked what he saw. He watched for her return and stepped out to walk along with her while he introduced himself. She was pleased at his manner and attention. He showed up to walk with her again and again.

One Saturday morning, at his suggestion, he and Lorna picked up some supplies at a local grocery store and went down to the creek south of town to have a picnic. They talked for a long time and watched the water flow by. She liked hearing about his work, which seemed quite exciting to a country girl with limited experience in the "big world." What they didn't realize was that their being seen together like this was causing stress in the social fabric of Sand Creek. She was married and a teacher. It just wasn't right. Someone got in touch with her husband and told him he had better get there soon to save his marriage.

In the meantime, *Boogus* decided that Arnie was causing too much trouble so he shipped him back to his old boarding school up north. The year was ending and so was everything else that was good in Gregg's life. Lorna's husband came in town on a three-day pass and made it clear that she was finished in Sand Creek. As the two of them were getting ready to leave, Gregg passed them by on a downtown street. He could tell she had been crying a lot. The emotional pain he felt at seeing her so hurt was overwhelming. He was also devastated by his own sense of loss. He was convinced that never again would anything good happen to him in that "stupid" town.

Breaking away

Another teenager that was just as fed up with life in Sand Creek as Gregg was came rushing up to him one day and said, "I have some great news. I just found out that they are so short of men in the Merchant Marines they're taking guys as young as sixteen. We can lie about our age a little and join up. As soon as we're sworn in, we can tell everybody around here to go to hell." So, Gregg and Don hitched rides to the nearest Merchant Marine recruiting station in Cincinnati, Ohio. The recruiting officer sensed that they were not yet sixteen and confronted them in private. He offered to help them get around that problem, if they would help him with something. He wanted them to get him two pages of farm implement ration stamps. If they brought him the (gasoline) stamps, he would postdate their enlistment papers and send them through. By the time anyone would notice their birth dates they would already be sixteen. He said that with seamen for merchant ships so badly needed nothing was likely to be done about the "mistake."

Back in Sand Creek, it was rather easy to get the two pages of gasoline ration stamps. Gregg and Don were friendly with another boy whose mother was head of the local rationing office. In each ration book she received from the government there was a fixed number of stamps. When it was determined how many stamps an applicant was to receive, all of the stamps above that number were removed from the book. The surplus stamps were stashed in a special box and her son was periodically sent out back of the office to burn them. The burn basket was in full view from a rear window of the rationing office. When his mother dropped her gaze or turned away to answer the phone, their friend was able to slip some of the stamps under a stone he had placed nearby. After the office was closed for the day he would return to remove the stamps from under the stone. With these arrangements, he was able to keep himself in spending money and have plenty of gas for his own car. He gave Gregg and Don a break on the price for two pages of "salvaged" stamps. He said he wished he were going with them. He was old enough to enlist in any branch of military service with parental permission, but his mother wouldn't sign for him. He was her only child and she was afraid he'd be killed in action. She wanted him to finish high school and go to college.

Stamps in hand, Gregg and Don went back to Cincinnati. They gave the stamps to the recruiting officer and he started the paperwork on their enlistments. Then they were sent to separate locations for physical exams. Gregg finished first and had just been sworn in when Don appeared with tears streaming down his face. He explained that the examiners found he had a heart murmur and they wouldn't approve him for active duty. Greg's heart sank. He was shocked. He felt terrible for his friend. Don was going back to Sand Creek where he desperately didn't want to be. Especially after being classified as unfit for service in the Merchant Marines. At least he would be around familiar faces. Gregg was going off to boot camp in New York City. Alone. Where he knew no one. Where he didn't have any idea what to expect. Real and deepening fear was added to his depression. He made the long train trip to boot camp in a daze.

Looking back on the circumstances that took him out of Sand Creek alone and placed him far away from everything familiar, he realized it probably was another (no coincidence) example of guided serendipity in his life. He retrieved the energy he had been giving over to frustration, foolishness, and protecting himself in the hostile environment of Sand Creek. He busied himself with learning how to do the new tasks at hand. Knot tying. Sailing. Handling shipboard fires. Survival techniques if dumped in the sea from a torpedoed ship. Identifying a ship's very numerous parts by name and function. How to fire the boilers for the giant steam engines. How to lubricate those engines by hand while they were hard at work. How to be a responsible member of a seafaring team. Because of his accomplishments in the routine program of instruction, he was sent to a special class on the various types of valves found on a ship. Still in boot camp, he had nothing to do but think and study after his classes were finished and he had done his laundry. He found that when he was so focused, learning about all of those specialized valves and their many uses on a ship was a breeze. When the final exam was given, his instructors were amazed to find that he had made the only perfect score ever achieved by a student in the class. At the boot camp graduation ceremonies he was given special recognition for this achievement.

In addition to the good feelings that came with this recognition for academic achievement, Gregg was aware that something else was happening within himself. He was gaining new respect for his ability to think and learn. Besides his high marks in the class on marine control valves, his company was selected to march in a parade down

Avenue of The Americas in New York City. The mayor had requested that two or three of the very best drill teams be sent to march in the parade. Gregg's team was selected from among many companies in training at the Brooklyn Base because of the consistent high quality of their precision executions of complicated drills. Marching down that grand boulevard in Manhattan was a thrilling experience. The cheering crowds, waving flags, and martial music sent his spirits soaring. It was also a turning point in his life. He was ready to focus on *serious learning* and go wherever that would take him. At the time, he fantasized that he was on his way to one day becoming Captain of a merchant ship.

After the indoctrination period of six weeks, Gregg and his fellow trainees were paid and given passes to go off the base on weekends. With money in their pockets and dressed in new uniforms, they found that the bars in New York City were happy to serve them. Gregg and a buddy who was straight off a farm in Iowa took full advantage of this new access to the "pleasures" of alcohol that were beyond the reach of sixteen year old boys in civilian life. They had little experience with it, except for an occasional swig of hard cider or home-brew beer allowed by an older friend or relative back home. Their first tastes of cold beer, ordered from a tap while standing at a very busy bar, weren't as good as expected. They figured it must be an off-brand or a batch rushed to market to take advantage of eager wartime consumers. They drank and moved on, in search of something better. After a few samples in a few different bars, everything tasted the same. They lost track of how many glasses they had and didn't care very much. In the wee hours of the morning, when their cash ran short, they headed back to the base. Once on the subway train to Sheepshead Bay in Brooklyn, they nodded off to a deep sleep induced by extreme fatigue and too much alcohol. As the train approached the base, a watchful conductor tried to rouse them. He was not successful. When the train stopped he dragged them out of the car and laid them on the platform. Some other sailors came by later, shook them until they responded, and told them they would be court-martialed if they arrived at the base too intoxicated to stay awake the next day. They held onto them while they "ran" a few blocks and then helped them get some black coffee at an all-night restaurant just outside the gate. Gregg and his buddy just got into their bunks when reveille was sounded. A few minutes later they were marching to breakfast, which they didn't really feel like eating. Then there was more marching to attend lectures in overheated classrooms. That was when the real pain set in. Their eyes felt like heavy lead weights. The siren song of blissful sleep was irresistible. They nodded forward like diving ducks. Someone called the Shore Patrol and they were escorted out to the hallway. There they were told that sitting would no longer be allowed. They had to stand against the rear wall and keep their eyes open at all times. If they went to sleep and lost their balance, they would be carted off to the brig. Extreme fear kept them awake through what seemed like endless hours of pure agony. They vowed that they would **never** get into such a miserable state again.

Another "night on the town" in New York City presented Gregg with a different problem. He was hanging around Times Square when a large group of good-looking young girls got off a subway train from Brooklyn. They went up to each of the sailors present and invited them to a dance in their neighborhood. When a sailor for each girl had been secured, they were led on a subway ride to the parochial school where the dance was being held. At first, it seemed like a very good deal. There was a big spread of good food and plenty of girls eager to dance. In fact, they were a little too eager. What he didn't know at the time was that the girls and their regular boy friends had been fighting. Picking up sailors in Times Square had been organized to get revenge. However, the displaced boys decided to "eject" the intruding sailors and make sure they would never come back. Gregg was in a rest room when he heard loud screaming and crying. He cautiously peered out to see what was the matter. A sailor that he knew was laid out on a table with girls wailing and hovering around him. They were trying to stop the bleeding from several wounds on his head and face. They were also cursing the neighborhood boys who were outside and looking for more sailors to "teach them a lesson." Gregg noticed a side door and asked a friendly girl if he could get out that way. She said it led to an alley behind the school and told him how to get from there to the closest subway station. "Stay in the shadows until you are at the end of the alley; then run for it. The guys know how many sailors came here with us. They'll soon notice you are missing and come in here to look for you. You can make it if you go right now and hurry." He followed her instructions and was within two blocks of the subway station when he heard them yelling and running after him. His old survival skill "kicked in" and he quickly increased the distance between himself and his pursuers. He arrived at the subway station just as a train was coming in. As his "nick-of-time" safety capsule pulled out of the station he saw the boys who were chasing after him appear on the platform. They were cursing him and yelling threats. He bypassed Times Square and went immediately back to the base. He thought to himself that someone or something was surely looking out for him. He wondered how and why.

CHAPTER III

Seminal Incubation

There are no mistakes, no coincidences. All events are blessings to learn from.

--- Elizabeth Kubler-Ross

After graduation from boot camp, Gregg was put on a train to Charleston, South Carolina. From there he was assigned to the engine room crew of an oil tanker that was making regular runs to and from Venezuela. To avoid being a lighted target for German submarines lurking off the coast, the ship's porthole windows were painted black and kept shut. The doorways were covered with double rows of heavy waterproof curtains to form a maze-like passageway so no light could escape. Garbage was only dumped overboard at midnight so the ship would be many miles away from any telltale floating debris when daylight arrived. As the great ship lumbered on toward the equator, the air in the sleeping quarters inside the ship grew unbearably warm and stale. The crew staked out places on the upper deck to put folding cots so they could sleep outside. Even so, Gregg had a bad case of prickly heat rash and was miserable with it until he got back to cooler and less humid air as the ship returned to Charleston.

Some intense and life changing events

On the way down to Venezuela he had a terrifying experience and almost lost his life. Two days out to sea they were hit by a major hurricane. The old oil tanker creaked and groaned as it bobbed up and down in the giant waves like a bottle cork. Gregg was somewhat reassured by an older sailor who told him that creaking and groaning was good. With a knowing grin he said, "If she's too stiff to creak and groan, she'll break up in a storm like this." Nevertheless, working in the engine room at the bottom of the ship when it sounded like it would come apart any minute took its toll. He was greatly relieved when his watch ended and he could go topside to try and get some sleep.

The old ship churned forward through the furious wind and rain. Enormous waves crashed across the lower decks fore and aft of the ship's bridge. After its cargo of oil was unloaded in Charleston, a lot of ocean water had been pumped into the empty tanks. It was needed to weigh the ship down and make it ride low enough to be stable in a churning ocean. With this saltwater ballast in its tanks the ship didn't ride quite as low as when it was filled with crude oil. However, most of its giant steel body was beneath the surface of the ocean at all times. In boot camp they had been warned to stay off the lower decks of an oil tanker when a storm watch was in effect. Being swept overboard by an unexpected and unforgiving wave was likely. Being rescued during storm conditions was not. The wisdom of that warning was reinforced when he learned that another member of the crew had been crossing a lower deck when the first big wave hit the ship. He was instantly swept overboard and never seen again.

As Gregg climbed to the upper deck, the storm began to quiet down and the ocean grew increasingly quieter. By the time he reached his cot under the big canvas tarp on the starboard side of the main deck, everything was calm and peaceful. He crawled onto his mattress and was soon sleeping soundly. He didn't realize that the calming was because the ship had moved into the eye of the hurricane. Later, the ship moved back out of the eye and was again met by the full fury of the storm. An enormous wave hit the ship broadside and almost turned it upside down. He was terrified to be jolted awake and find that his cot was sliding rapidly down the steeply tilted deck. Instinctively, he reached out for the railing as his cot and clothing disappeared over the side and into the raging ocean. He clung tightly to the railing while the ship hesitated at the peak of its roll and then dropped back down into the deep trough of another wave with a resounding crash. Hanging on to anything solid that he could reach, he scrambled for a doorway and went inside. He was shaking badly and felt the urge to vomit. *He had been a few seconds away from certain death.*

Eventually, the storm subsided. The sun reappeared with a fiery vengeance. Everything on board the old tanker settled down to monotonous routines. Greg was assigned to duty in the engine room everyday from 4: 00 pm to 8:00 pm and again from 4:00 am to 8:00 am. When he started his watch the first order of business was to make coffee and deliver it to the First Engineer at his quarters two decks above. The coffee had to be steaming hot. It was made in a coffee pot heated by steam produced in the giant engine boilers. When brewed coffee was drawn from the pot into a heavy ceramic cup, it was heated again by releasing more steam (expresso like) into the liquid. The too-hot-to-handle cup was then placed on a tray and carried up to the First Engineer. He expected it exactly ten minutes after the duty period began. He would immediately answer a knock on the door and take the blistering hot coffee without a word. Then he would drink it down without batting an eye and order a second cup. That astonishing behavior along with many other stories about his steely toughness caused the men under his command to fear him a great deal. They did their best to avoid coming to his attention and activating his legendary wrath.

After the coffee was made and delivered, there were burner tubes to be cleaned and made ready for inspection. The fireman on duty was responsible for removing one burner tube from each of the

41

three massive boilers and replacing them with tubes cleaned by the previous watch crew. Then he would spend the rest of his duty time watching gauges and adjusting valves to keep the steam pressure exactly to the degree ordered by the First Engineer. Not a little above or a little below, but right on the line. It was a task that required the fireman's full attention at all times.

After helping the fireman to clean the dirty burner tubes, Gregg was sent to oil the crankshaft bearings on the enormous three-cylinder steam engine. The crankshaft was not enclosed and oiling it was done with a hand-held squirt can. In the engine school at boot camp he had learned how to concentrate and do this maneuver in synchronized rhythm with the rotating shaft. One careless move could easily break an oiler's arm by pinning it between the solid steel piers supporting the cylinders and pistons overhead. After oiling the engine, he spent the rest of his "watch" on the never-ending task of cleaning (wiping) the metal surfaces in the engine room. The danger and boredom of this work convinced him that it was time to get back to *serious learning* so he could pass the prescribed exams for higher rank. He went to the ship's library and checked out the requirements and a study manual for the rank of First Class Seaman, which was the next step up the ladder.

As he was looking over the study materials, it suddenly came to him that he could achieve his *serious learning* goal and improve his standing with the First Engineer at the same time and by the same efforts. He decided that he would ask this well-educated and very experienced man to quiz him on his understanding of the study materials before he took a test. Never mind that going to see him with this unprecedented request would be like sticking his head in a lion's mouth. His intuition told him that guts and sincerity would win the Engineer's approval. He crossed the deck and knocked on the door to his quarters as he had done many times before when delivering superheated coffee.

"Well, what the hell do you want?"

"Sir, I wonder if I could have a few minutes of your time."

"Something screwed up in the engine room?"

"No sir, I have…"

"You in some kind of trouble, boy?"

"No sir. I have something I'd like to talk with you about. If you have few minutes. It won't take very long."

"Well, don't stand out there. Come in and let me have it. This better not be something stupid."

"Thank you…"

"Just spit it out boy, I haven't got all day."

"Well, I've started studying what it takes to make the next rank. I already know from the stuff they taught us at boot camp that it's good as far as it goes but when you're on a real ship out to sea there's a lot more to it than the words in a book can tell."

"That's for damn sure. Some real important things you can only learn by experience on a ship. Any idiot knows that much. Get on with what you came here for."

"Yes sir. Well, I know you must have had lots of experience on all kinds of ships to get to be a First Engineer. You can see where the stuff in the study manual is missing something important. I already know I can learn what's in the book and pass the test. But I really want to learn what I need to do the job right. I was wondering if you would be willing to quiz me on what I'm studying. So you could help me fill in the gaps between what's in the book and what I really need to know. Before I go for the test."

"You want me to be your goddamned tutor? What makes you think I give a shit about whether you pass the fucking test or not?"

"Well, sir. I know you care about your work on this ship. You want it done on time and you want it done right. It's not just any old job to you. If you could give me the benefit of your experience on this, I can do more than just get ready to pass a test. I can learn something in the process that will help me be a better crew member."

(After a very long pause) "All right, dammit, we'll give it a try. Come to my quarters every evening at exactly 7:00 pm. Be on time. I'll give you thirty minutes. Be ready to show me what you have learned from that book. And be sure you've covered enough material between meetings to make it worth my time. Don't fool around with me or you'll be sorry you ever started this."

"Thank you sir. I'm really serious and I'll be ready. I really appreciate it that you'll help me with this."

Over time, the "ferocious" First Engineer saw that Gregg was truly serious. He tested him extensively and added much to his understanding with real life examples. Their relationship mellowed. A few days before the ship got back to port in Charleston, Gregg took the official test and passed "with flying colors." He was elated because of his educational achievement and the approval he got from his unorthodox tutor.

Flush with success in his *serious learning* ventures, he went back to the ship's library for the next set of study guides. He would try to get certified for the rank of Third Class Petty Officer. It was the next level up from the First Class Seaman rank he had just achieved. What he found in these study guides instantly took the wind out of his sails. A *high school diploma was required for any rank above First Class Seaman.*

While stressing about this dilemma, he was surprised to get some very important help from another "old salt." His qualifications to advise a naïve young man like Gregg were gained from many years at sea. He had traveled all over the world. In each port of call he spent his earnings on women and booze. He would stagger, or be delivered, back to his ship with his money spent and feeling like he had been hit by a truck. Sleep it off and then go back to work at a level far below where he would be without such behavior. A devastating cycle that he had repeated countless times. He pulled Gregg aside and told him his story. He said he had been just like Gregg when he left a good home and went to sea. Easy money. Easy women. Easy booze. No one to tell him not to do it. Somewhere along the way he got addicted and lost himself. He told Gregg to take a good look at him. Then he said, "You don't belong in this kind of life. Get your ass back home and finish high school before it's too late. There's nothing good for you here. You can't even get out of the engine room without a high school education." His words stung sharply, but Gregg *knew* they were words of wisdom. He made his decision right then to continue his *serious learning* back in high school. When the ship docked in Charleston, and his duty commitment was finished, he took the first available train back to Sand Creek.

Gregg returned to his old hometown and went back to high school under nearly impossible conditions. He had missed the last three weeks of his junior year. His original class group was already six weeks into their senior year. He wanted to make up the work he had missed and continue along with them. The principal was new on the job and said he didn't have enough background information to make such a decision without consulting the faculty. He told Gregg he would present his request at a faculty meeting that afternoon. "Come back to my office tomorrow morning and I'll let you know what we can do."

When the teachers heard that Gregg wanted to come back to school, they were unanimous in expressing resistance to letting a known troublemaker back on the premises. Especially after he had been "out in the big world" where he surely learned things that were not good for the inexperienced kids in their school to know about. However, on the basis of the principal's report that he found Gregg truly repentant and wanting to be a *serious learner,* the faculty reluctantly agreed that he could return if he accepted certain conditions. The conditions they set up were quite harsh. Partly punitive for his past transgressions. Partly to discourage him from even trying. They were designed to avoid any problems if Gregg did meet them (which they doubted that he would) and to quickly get rid of him if he didn't.

Must achieve a grade of A in deportment or conduct; any deviation at anytime will result in automatic termination without appeal.

Must make at least a B average in all courses.

Must write a composition for each class missed during the
nine weeks of classes not attended.

No grades will be issued until the last day of the school
year. You will only know you are doing OK if you are not
told to pack up and leave.

The teachers hoped he would look at these conditions and realize
he wouldn't be able to abide by them. They were shocked when he
accepted the plan and said that he deeply appreciated the opportunity.
They also predicted his imminent failure.

Besides his recent learning successes in the Merchant Marines
boot camp and in studying with the First Engineer on the ship, Gregg
had some other vital supports in this learning quest. The County
Superintendent's daughter, who had been a friend and confidant since
grade school, told him he definitely could do it. She also mobilized
a small group of classmates who helped him with his homework
and constantly reminded him he could be a winner. They talked to
the Social Studies teacher about his abilities and convinced her to
encourage his exceptional thinking. That teacher soon developed
a genuine appreciation for his contributions to the class. She let
him know it by calling on him a lot and engaging him in high level
discussions. Writing all of those compositions was a real pain for him
and a condition that backfired on the teachers who almost gleefully
created it. They had to provide all of the lesson topics. He wrote
several compositions each weekend and submitted them on Mondays.
And they had to carefully read them all to evaluate his work. This
procedure was painful for everyone. However, most of the teachers
involved were favorably impressed as they reviewed his compliant
and competent work.

Probably the single most powerful support came from the
principal. Besides being an educator, he was an ordained minister.
He strongly believed in helping those who showed signs of wanting to
help themselves. He was a kind and compassionate man. He realized
that Gregg was in a vulnerable position and devised his own plan to

give him vital assistance. He asked Gregg to come to his office once each week to talk about how things were going. During one of these sessions, he said he had an overwhelming backlog of reports to fill out for the State Superintendent's Office. Some of them had been left unfinished by his predecessor who was drafted. He wondered if Gregg would be interested in earning a little pocket money by helping him get caught up. The offer was quickly accepted. Did he realize it was a manufactured job? Yes! Was it a good deal? Yes! The close working relationship did provide a little spending money, which he desperately needed. It also offered some insulation from arbitrary actions by a few teachers who were less than enchanted with his presence in the school. Certainly, it was a big factor in keeping him on the right path and out of trouble.

Without the principal's help, he definitely would have gone down the tubes on one occasion in the science class that Mr. Anderson taught from the book (or his interpretation of what he found there). During a lesson on engines he explained that steam engines were reciprocating engines and gasoline engines were internal combustion engines. Having completed engine school in the Merchant Marines a few months earlier, Gregg thought he would be helpful and point out that gasoline engines were also classified as reciprocating engines because of the back and forth (reciprocating) movement of their pistons. Mr. Anderson did not receive the information as helpful. In fact, he was furious. He said that he was teaching the class and ordered Gregg out of the room. He told him to wait in the hall until the class was over and he would talk to him then. When the bell rang, the other students quickly left the room and Mr. Anderson came out to where Gregg was standing.

"Pack up your things. You are through in this school. I will personally see that you never graduate."

"I'm really sorry sir; I really didn't mean to cause any trouble. I was just sharing what I learned in engine school. I thought it would be helpful."

"Listen; nobody corrects me in my class. I'm the one that's getting paid to teach. You've mouthed off one time too many. It's over for you. Just get the hell out of here and save yourself a lot of trouble."

"Isn't there anything I can do to convince you that I am truly sorry and didn't mean to cause a problem? I really want to finish school and I have been trying very hard to live up to all of the conditions I was given when I came back."

"Listen; try to get this in your head. You are done here. You are wasting your time. I'm on your case and I say you are finished."

Then the enraged teacher went back into his classroom and firmly closed the door. Gregg was devastated. His plan to be a *serious learner* was about to go down the drain because one egotistical and insecure person took a valid contribution the wrong way. He didn't imagine that Mr. Anderson would take his comment as an attempt to show that he was unqualified to teach the course. At that moment the principal passed by and saw the distress on his face. He motioned for Gregg to come into his office. He wanted to know what had happened. When Gregg told him, he said to wait there in his office while he talked with Mr. Anderson. About thirty minutes later he returned and said, "Go back to class tomorrow. Keep quiet and do whatever you are told by Mr. Anderson. Don't offer any information he doesn't directly ask of you. Study hard and keep your test scores up. I promise that if you do that, and keep up the good work you have been doing in all of your other classes, you will graduate." A very close call! When the year ended and he finally got a report card, his grades looked like those of a real student. He knew there would be nothing less than a B, because he hadn't been asked to leave. He was amazed and very pleased to find that most of his grades were A's.

Gregg was also aware that he had actually learned some important things; especially in the Social Studies class where the teacher constantly challenged him. She, too, had been pressed into service because of the wartime teacher shortage. She had left teaching several years earlier to be a homemaker and raise her family. It was clear that she loved teaching and the stimulation of encouraging young people to examine important ideas. He was grateful for her decision to come back to the classroom just when he could benefit from her knowledge and teaching skills. Another case of guided serendipity? Not really a coincidence? And what about the principal? He was only at the school for two years. The first of those was Gregg's year of "nearly impossible" return and personal challenge. How was it that this special man appeared on the scene at this very critical time in his life and that made all the difference?

The letdown after graduation was enormous. He had come to enjoy the stimulation of *serious learning.* Then he heard that Lorna's husband had been killed in action. He had very mixed feelings about that. Some relief. Some regret. Concern and depression about what she must be going through. Lingering distress about his status in Sand Creek without the protective cocoon of his high school support group. The principal had gone back home to his northern Indiana farm for the summer. And the Marshall was still on his case. Looking for solace and some replacement action got him back into military service, first in the National Guard and then in the U.S. Navy.

He learned from a friend that someone he knew in the Merchant Marines was back home in Rockton for a visit between duty tours. A phone call was made and they set up a meeting for a beer or two while "old salts" traded seafaring tales. Their slightly embellished stories caused them both to become unreasonably eager for more maritime adventures. Their overwhelming nostalgia for life on a ship was probably bolstered by their deep sense of boredom and a little too much beer. A deal was struck. In two weeks they would go up to the Maritime Union Hall in New York City and apply for new shipboard assignments. After scraping up all the cash they could earn, beg, or borrow, they said their goodbyes and took a bus from Rockton to Indianapolis. They bought train tickets there and were soon on their way to seek new maritime adventures.

After arriving in New York City and securing a room at a nearby YMCA, Gregg and Malcolm went over to the Union Hall to see what was available. Some good prospects were up on the boards.

Several ships that needed crewmembers would arrive in the next few days. They made some notes and went back to the "Y" for a snooze before going out on the town. That evening they were standing on the sidewalk in Times Square when something unexpected and very special intervened in their lives. There, in big bright letters moving around the electronic billboard on the Times Building, was the unmistakable message that the war with Japan had ended! V-J Day! Pandemonium! All hell broke loose! Drivers of trucks and cars, including the infamous New York taxicabs, moved quickly to vacate the streets around the square. They had some experience with what took place there on a New Year's Eve. They knew that would certainly be exceeded by activities to celebrate the end of a terrible war. People poured out of buildings. There was spontaneous hugging and kissing everywhere. The bars opened their taps and kept the beer flowing. A few cars didn't make it out immediately and were "captured" by the mob-like crowd. People piled on to the blocked cars and stood on every available surface. Tires blew out. Trunks and roofs and hoods were crushed. They were sacrificed to the celebration. Soon, thousands of people were in Times Square and the surrounding side streets. Bodies were so tightly packed that independent movement was not possible. People went wherever the crowd took them. Gregg was soon separated from his maritime buddy. After being pushed back and forth in the increasingly dangerous crowd for thirty or forty minutes, he climbed up a lamp post and sat on a NYPD call box. While clinging to that uncomfortable perch he was handled, rubbed, bumped, hugged, and kissed. At least he was relatively safe. He learned the next day that others in that crowd were not so fortunate. They had lost their footing when the crowd pushed them over a fire-plug, or some other unyielding obstacle, and they were trampled to death by feet that couldn't be stopped.

It was near daylight the next morning before the crowd thinned out enough for him to get down from his perch and wend his way back to the "Y." His buddy came in a short time later. They were both totally exhausted. They quickly "crashed" and slept like the dead for the next ten or twelve hours. On awakening, they could already hear that the celebration was still under way and revving up as darkness approached. They quickly showered and dressed. Then they went down to join the revelry. The second night went pretty much like the first. When Gregg awoke the next day, he found that he had a ring of bright red kiss prints all around his midriff. He didn't remember anything at all about how they got there. In that pressurized crowd of people, with his awareness dimed by abundant free beer, he allowed that it could have happened as he was being "transported" around the square. For several hours the third night of celebrating was much like the first two and then the crowd began to thin out. A few taxi drivers cautiously approached the square and started picking up bleary-eyed customers. Gregg and Malcolm took stock of their money. There wasn't much left. They decided it was time to stop celebrating and get some rest so they could check in at the Union Hall the next day. They still weren't feeling very well when they arrived at the Hall. They soon felt worse when they inquired about jobs on incoming ships. With the Japanese surrender, the great World War II effort was finished. Except for bringing men and materiel back home, the need for transporting things by ship was greatly reduced. The extreme shortage of men to operate the ships no longer existed. The available jobs would be going to older and more experienced men. Unpredictable teen-agers were cut from the application lists.

Gregg and Malcolm realized that except for their experience of celebrating the war's end in Times Square, they were going back to Sand Creek empty handed. Their next problem was how to get there. They didn't have enough money left for train tickets. They also realized that going back under these circumstances would oblige them to eat a lot of crow followed by ample dessert of humble pie. They hated to be going home to that, but there was no better choice. They went to the Western Union Office and spent their last few dollars on telegrams to folks back home asking that they wire them money for train tickets. With no money left, they had to spend the next twelve hours in the Western Union waiting room, until the operator told them their cash had arrived.

For the same reasons that the maritime jobs in New York City had disappeared, jobs of any kind back home were rapidly vanishing. Many factories that had been working overtime to produce war materiel were using only skeleton crews to retool for production of civilian goods. Veterans returning from military service were being given first priority for employment. Under these circumstances, Gregg and several of his friends responded to a new recruiting effort by the National Guard. The pay wasn't much but the members got to wear a uniform. Every Wednesday night they met at the Armory in Milltown for marching drills and training classes. They also took part in maneuvers at a nearby military base every other weekend. The best part of the maneuvers was firing a variety of guns at the rifle range. Especially fifty caliber machine guns with tracer bullets after dark. After a few weeks even that got monotonous. The only time they had any real excitement was when they were called out of a movie in Milltown and told to report to the Armory for emergency action. The emergency action turned out to threatening actions by striking workers at the Standard Oil Refinery in Whiting, Indiana. They loaded guns and other riot equipment into several armored vehicles and started north. Somewhere near the city of Anderson they got the word that he strike had been settled. So they turned around and headed back to Milltown. Back to routines of marching in formation, repetitive training classes, cleaning guns, shooting at the rifle range, and maneuvers every other weekend.

One night the Company Commander made a very interesting announcement. The Guard was cooperating with the Navy to offer a special program. Current members of the Guard who were seventeen could transfer to the Navy for a minority enlistment (until they were twenty-one). Gregg and four other boys answered the call. They were soon on their way to (another) boot camp near Williamsburg, Virginia.

When Gregg finished boot camp, he was assigned to duty in one of the fire stations on the base. This assignment gave him the time and opportunity to get started again with his *serious learning.* He went to the Education Office on the base and checked out study materials for moving up in rank. After his study experience with the First Engineer on the old oil tanker, getting ready to take the Navy tests was a breeze. During the next several weeks, he passed the required tests for the next two Seaman ranks and the rank of Third Class Petty Officer. These achievements were duly entered into his service record. And he was selected to go for several weeks of special training at the Navy's school for shipboard fire control in Norfolk, Virginia. With that training and the requisite academic test already passed, he was promoted to the Petty Officer rank of Specialist Firefighter Third Class. Then the word came that the base was going to be decommissioned and taken out of service. Over the next few weeks, equipment and personnel were removed from the base and sent to other Navy installations. Only skeleton crews for property maintenance and fire prevention remained. Some of the fire station personnel requested and were given transfers to other bases or sea duty. Gregg was among those who elected to stay. Because he was the only firefighter remaining on the base that could type, he was moved from his berth at Able Station to the big main office at the Headquarters Station. There he struggled to keep the necessary paperwork moving and serve as equipment/personnel dispatcher whenever a fire call came in.

A big part of the paperwork was preparation of documents for personnel who were going on liberty. In this capacity, he had to deal with a variety of "creative" liberty requests and consult the regulations that applied. Before long he discovered a way to combine a couple of seventy-two hour passes so he and others could make long trips back to homes that were normally out of reach. On one of these trips back to Sand Creek, Gregg met the young woman that would soon become his wife.

Ellen and Greg met at an "open" steak-fry party at a private lake near Sand Creek. Anyone who heard about it and brought their own "supplies" was welcome to join the party. She arrived with someone who proceeded to drink too much beer too fast and passed out cold. Gregg offered to take her home after the party and she agreed. They quickly decided that they liked each other. His invitation to go with him and some friends to a movie in Rockton the next evening was also accepted. Both of them were very needy people. They found mutual relief from painful loneliness in huddling with each other in the darkness of the theater and on the long ride back to Sand Creek. That was the beginning of a relationship that caused them both to experience a great deal of distress when he had to go back to his Navy assignment in far away Virginia. In a series of desperate letters they planned to get married the next time he could find a way to meet her somewhere between his base and Sand Creek. To earn money for the trip, he set up a "business" in the fire station, pressing dress uniforms for other sailors. By working whenever he wasn't on duty or getting a few hours of sleep, he soon accumulated enough cash to cover the costs for their transportation to Cincinnati and a civil ceremony. He sent her a train ticket with instructions to meet him in the lobby of the Cincinnati train station the following Saturday. Then he called her to confirm that she would be there and ready to "tie the knot." She happily replied that she would be there "with bells on."

After meeting in Cincinnati they went across the river to a well-known marriage mill in Covington, Kentucky. Since she was seventeen and he was barely eighteen, the minister was supposed to require proof of parental permission. Gregg called one of his buddies in Virginia and had him send a telegram to the minister that simply stated, "I give my permission for my son's marriage. (signed) Mom." Ellen called one of her aunts who agreed to tell the minister that she was acting in place of Ellen's mother who was deceased and that she approved of the marriage to Gregg. Although anyone other than a marriage mill minister who wanted the business would have been skeptical of these approvals, they were accepted and the deed was done.

After a night in a Cincinnati hotel they traveled by train and bus back to Sand Creek. They had agreed that after they were married Ellen would stay at his grandmother's house in Sand Creek until she finished high school. That turned out to be a promise she was unable to keep. She was miserable living there without him. She was too depressed to study. She fell behind in her schoolwork. She was soon begging him to let her come to Virginia and get a job near the base. Out of his sympathy for her feelings of deep despair and his own loneliness he finally gave in. A short time after she arrived in Virginia, they learned that she was pregnant. Gregg was very concerned about how they would cope with this unplanned situation. There was the issue of a money shortage when she would no longer be able to work. As her pregnancy progressed, she would be alone in a rented apartment many miles from any family that could visit with her or give her a hand. He would be on duty at the Fire Station at the base and unavailable except for some weekends. He was afraid that these circumstances would be harmful for his wife and development of the baby.

Then something unexpected intervened. Soon after VJ Day signaled the end of hostile actions in both major war theaters, the Navy Commanders had begun to think about ways to reduce the number of unneeded personnel on active duty. One result of their deliberations was a plan that was a major blessing for Gregg and his pregnant wife. Enlisted men with serious family problems could apply for a dependency discharge. Gregg's circumstances enabled him to make a strong case for release from his original service commitment. Within three weeks after submitting his application, he was mustered out of the Navy. He and Ellen headed back to Sand Creek and a very uncertain future.

Although jobs around Sand Creek were very scarce, he had an "ace in the hole" at a big diesel engine factory in Milltown. One of his uncles (by marriage) was in a high-level management position there.

He agreed to see that Gregg's application was approved for a job somewhere in his department. Some of his Navy severance pay was used to buy work clothes and a lunch bucket. Things were looking up. He went in for a personal interview and a physical exam, confident that he would be earning good money for his family very soon. That never happened. The X-ray pictures taken during his exam showed some scar tissue on his lungs. The doctor said that he scars might have resulted from the mild pneumonia he had in Navy boot camp or exposure to some other type of toxic agent. He really couldn't tell. However, with a history of tuberculosis in his family there was concern that they might be lesions caused by exposure to the *tubercle bacillus* in his childhood home. Under those circumstances, insurance regulations would not allow the Company to hire him.

Wiped out! Lifted to the heights and then smashed to the ground. With a baby on the way. He was too demoralized to see if he could convince some other factory to hire him in spite of his slightly scarred lungs. Following a tip from friends, he was able to find work as a laborer on a low-paying construction job in Sand Crcek. It kept food on the table. He also started working part-time in a local grocery store. He managed the store by himself on Sunday mornings. While it didn't pay much either, it was a job he liked and found vital to getting through the next "impossible" phase of his life.

Rescued by an unexpected and timely intervention

Sometime during that summer the County Nurse, who watched over the young people in her district like a mother hen, invited him into her office for a talk. She asked him lots of questions about his family situation and what job prospects he had on tap. He shared his very disappointing recent experience at the Diesel engine factory. He was clearly depressed at his prospects. At the conclusion of much friendly exchange she told him that he should stop looking for a job and go to college. She said that with his family medical history it was important for him to have a job away from metal particles or dust that could irritate his lungs. She also said that because he had served in the military he could get some help through a new program called the G.I. Bill. "It won't be easy, but it is a way to have a better life." She gave him the address of an office in Milltown where he could get the full details. He went with one of his buddies who had been with him in the National Guard and the Navy. What they learned in that meeting profoundly changed both their lives. When the agent asked them what they wanted to study in college, they were at a loss. He advised them to do what a number of other applicants had done. "Go into education. Get a degree and a teacher's license. You'll be able to earn a decent living and look after your families while you decide what you really want to do." They took the agent's wise counsel and were soon two struggling college students with "barebones" financial assistance from the G.I. Bill program.

Extraordinary events offer new perspectives

Two special things happened to Gregg while he was living in Sand Creek and commuting to the University in Rockton. They happened because of extraordinary attributes he was developing in a part of himself beyond his conscious awareness. At the time, he saw them as ordinary events that could happen to anybody. He felt he just happened to be there at the right time and thinking the right way. In his view, he was a little creative and a lot lucky.

The first of these experiences involved "Aunt Mamie." She was the wife of his grandfather's twin brother and matriarch of a large branch of Gregg's extended family. She and her husband lived in an old log cabin up a "holler" off Crooked Valley Road. Her own immediate family of seven children had long since grown up and moved out of the nest. Most of them built their own homes on other parcels of the family land. A few ventured to build on some new land purchased as close by as possible. Only the oldest daughter went off to find fame and fortune in the big city. She had been gone for many years, without much communication with folks back home. The family rarely discussed her situation and then only in the hushed tones used when telling deeply troublesome secrets.

Aunt Mamie's leadership in the family was due to her native wisdom and unusual appearance. Her face was deeply lined from years of bearing children and hard work in the fields of their marginal farm. She had lost her teeth years ago and refused to wear "store bought" dental plates. When she emerged from the dark interior of her old cabin in the dusky shadows of early evening or a cloudy day, she could easily have been taken for a witch. She was irrationally feared by some and respected by most. That only added to her mystique. A mystique that she put into good use as a *"natural borned healer."*

Aunt Mamie's healing specialty was curing warts. For miles around she was known as "that old woman who can cure warts." Her "practice" included animals as well as people. Many farmers gave testimony to her success with removing warts from the udders of their cows. She would tell them to leave the cow with her for a couple of days until she had time to "work on it." By the time they returned for the animal, the troublesome warts had disappeared. When people wanted warts removed from their own bodies, she would take them alone into her old dark cabin for about an hour. At the end of their treatment, she would tell them to go home and forget about the warts. "They'll go away as soon as you get your mind off of them." And they did!

A boy who lived near Sand Creek once had about fifteen warts on one hand. He was otherwise a handsome kid, about thirteen years old. He was so embarrassed by his "deformed" hand that he avoided contact with girls and kept his hand in his pocket most of the time. He and his family had tried many remedies without success. They even tied a dead cat on a string and had him swing it over his head in a graveyard at midnight like Tom Sawyer did. The pesky warts didn't change a bit. Gregg suggested that he let Aunt Mamie try to cure his warts. With a little pressure from some friends and his brothers (who were tired of hearing him complain) Jack let Gregg take him out to see Aunt Mamie. The day they went was overcast and the cabin seemed darkly foreboding. When Aunt Mamie appeared at the door, the look on Jack's face made it clear he would just as soon forget the whole thing. "Just leave him here with me and come back in about an hour." About two weeks later Gregg saw Jack with one of his brothers on the street in downtown Sand Creek. He asked how the warts were doing. "Nothing's changed. They are right where they were before I went out to that old witch's house." Then he pulled his hand out of his pocket to show Gregg the hated warts. But his hand was completely clean and smooth. Not a trace of where the warts had been. He quickly felt in his pocket to see if they had fallen off there. Nothing. "But they were all there when I went to bed last night." Then he and his brother got into their car and went home to see if maybe they had fallen off in the bed. They found nothing!

One day Aunt Mamie called Gregg and asked him to come up to her cabin because she had something for him. When he arrived, she invited him to stay for dinner (her term for the noontime meal). She had a roaring fire going in the old wood-burning cook stove. She prepared their food while she talked about "life." She made cornbread every day. Her recipe was in her head. She poured a "bunch' of hot lard into a big iron mixing pot. Next, she used her hand to scoop "some" corn meal into the pot. Then she pumped some water with the pitcher pump at the sink and added that to the pot. Finally, she added a little sugar and some salt to the mixture. When that was thoroughly stirred she poured it into a battered old baking pan and shoved it into the dancing hot oven. Talking all the while. No timers. No peeks to see how it was coming along. Several minutes later, she took the pan out of the oven and placed it in a cooler area on top of the stove. Gregg braved a look to see what had happened to the bread they would have for dinner (lunch). It was golden brown and crusty. Absolute perfection. Ingredients coaxed to a most harmonious blending by high order intuition and very experienced hands. It was served with "soup beans" and fresh sliced tomatoes. Gregg filled his plate twice and savored every bite.

After their meal together, she said she had made an important decision. She had "studied" everybody in the family to see who might be able to receive her gift for healing and use it to do good. She had finally settled on two people; Gregg and her youngest son, Arthur. She had already taught Arthur and now she wanted to teach Gregg. Arthur was about the same age as Gregg and they had always been good friends. They were more like brothers than first cousins, once removed. He figured that if Arthur had the "teaching" and survived, he could have it too. So that afternoon Aunt Mamie passed her gift along to him in a most serious and reverent manner. He didn't understand much of what she did at the time. He could feel her intentions for him immersed in a heartfelt prayer that she chanted while holding and stroking his hands. He thought that must have been the mumbling that Jack had reported when he got the treatment for his warts. He felt honored and somewhat uncertain. Several years went by before he tried to use the gift she gave him. And even then he bolstered his efforts with a scientific rationale to support what he was doing. It was a very long time after that before he came to understand the power of intentionality in prayers to effect healing.

Pre-cognitive knowing and remote viewing

The other special thing that happened that summer also involved a lot of *knowing/intuition,* only this time it was all his. Thinking back on it in the context of pre-cognitive and remote viewing phenomena, he realized the event was elicited by his exceptional sensitivities. For years he had heard stories of a mysterious secret cave. It was supposed to be on a wooded hillside somewhere near Sand Creek. He had asked many different people about it. The answers he received were always vague and uncertain about where it might be located. However, everyone he talked with said they truly believed that it existed. Little by little, bits and pieces of the stories pointed to a certain farm situated in a small valley about five miles east of the town. The property included wooded hills on either side of a few acres of tillable land in the valley between them. The owner was a very old man who listened patiently to Gregg's inquiries and confirmed that there was a cave entrance on the eastern hillside. He wouldn't tell where it was. The somber look on his weathered face slowly changed to a knowing grin like that displayed by the Cheshire Cat of *Alice In Wonderland.* He spat a stream of brown tobacco juice and said, "You can look all you want to but you'll never find it. It was closed up with big rocks and covered over with dirt a long time ago. That was done to keep people and animals from fallin' in it. Just don't leave my gates open or ride my fences down." Then he stopped talking and resumed his somber expression. After a long pause he said, "Besides there's Indian spirits in that cave and if anyone ever goes in it he won't come out alive." That only made Gregg more determined than ever to find the cave and explore it someday. With the old man's confirmation of the cave's existence and permission granted to make a "useless" search, he got really excited at the prospect of being the one who finally solved the mystery of the secret cave on the hill. He wandered the hillside for the next two days. He divided the sloping terrain into a grid and crisscrossed it carefully until he was certain he had covered every square foot. He found nothing that even remotely resembled the entrance to a cave. Then he got a brilliant idea. He went to the Department of Geology at the state university in Rockton and asked for their assistance in locating the cave. He knew they had located and explored many caves near the university campus. Their geological survey maps indicated that the bedrock around the campus was limestone. That was the kind of bedrock that lent itself to the formations of caves. When rainwater passed through the vegetation above it became slightly acidic. The acid water seeped into cracks and slowly dissolved the limestone to form cavities and tunnels below the surface. Eventually these were enlarged to form channels for underground creeks and even rivers. This kind of bedrock extended only a few miles east of the campus. Then it changed to sandstone. The whole county in which Sand Creek was located had a base of sandstone. The professors at the Department of Geology told him that he would not find any caves in the territory around Sand Creek because sandstone didn't dissolve like limestone. They said the story about a secret cave was only a creative legend without basis in fact. Powerful evidence, right? Time to pack it up and go home, right? Experts at a Big Ten university said it couldn't be true. In spite of all the evidence to the contrary, Gregg had a *knowing* insight that the cave did exist and he could find it.

Shortly after entering the university as a student, Gregg was asked to serve as leader of the Sand Creek Boy Scouts. All of the boys in his troop were very interested in learning about the Indians who had lived in the hills and valleys around their town. When they camped out in the woods they imagined what it was like to be a native Indian. Now and then they dressed like Indians and played games in the woods as if they were real Indians. They built campfires at night and told mysterious stories about the Indians. In the dark woods around the campfires it sometimes got so scary they were afraid to let the fire die down and go to sleep. One night when they were telling stories at their camp in the deep woods things got more scary and mysterious than ever before. The only light was from the campfire. It was just right for telling ghost stories and especially ghost stories about the Indians. Gregg listened for a long time. He could tell that the boys were both scared and excited. When they seemed about to run out of scary and mysterious stories to tell he offered to tell them about the secret cave on the hill. The boys got very quiet as he started to tell the story. He made up some mysterious things to relate it to the Indians the boys liked to hear about. He told them what the owner had said about it being cursed and if anyone ever went in it they wouldn't come out alive. He even speculated that the curse might be to protect a treasure the Indians had hidden there. When he said it all took place not far from where they were camped he expected them to get very scared. To his surprise, they acted just the opposite. They started asking questions.

"Where is this farm located?"

"On the road to little blue creek. About three miles from here."

"How many hills are on it?

"Only two. One on each side of the valley. The one on the east side is where the cave is supposed to be."

"Would the owner let us look for the cave if you went with us?"

"Yes. If we are careful not to ride his fences down or let his cows get out."

Would you help us try to find it?"

"Sure."

"What if we do find the cave? Would the entrance be big enough for us to get in?"

"I'm not sure about the size of the opening. We'll have to do some digging anyway because the owner said it had been filled in with rocks and dirt to keep animals and people from falling in it."

"What if we find that the Indians hid gold in the cave? Will it be cursed? Will there be Indian spirits in the cave? What will happen if we try to bring the gold out of the cave?"

Gregg didn't answer the last several questions they asked. He left their words hanging in the air to add to the mystery and to enlist the Troop's help in finding the cave. The boys got more and more excited. They convinced themselves that there was no such thing as Indian spirits in the cave. They felt sure there were scientific explanations for things that happened to people who looked for the cave when they were superstitious or scared. They begged Gregg to lead a search party and he said he would.

Early one morning Gregg and the boys in his troop started to search for the cave. Each boy had a long sharp stick to punch into leaf piles and under places where rocks stuck out of the sides of the hill. They hoped to find a soft spot and push their stick through it to find the entrance to the cave. They searched all morning and then had lunch. They searched all afternoon and then sat down for a late snack. One of the boys started to punch his stick into some leaves in a low place where a dead tree was uprooted by the wind. To his amazement, the stick pushed through and didn't hit anything hard. The boys scrambled to their feet and dug away at the leaves. Soon they knew they had found the cave.

The next day was a school day. The boys could hardly wait for 3:30 p.m. so they could go back to the secret cave. It was about 5:00 p.m. when they started up the hill. The leaves and brush were quickly removed from the opening to the cave entrance. At first the digging was easy. They cleared the tunnel right up to the big sharp rock in the middle. When they tried to dig around the rock they found that it got bigger and bigger the deeper they went. It was soon clear that it was much too big to dig loose and pry out. They were about to give up when one boy said he thought he could break off enough so someone could squeeze around it. Using one small ax for a chisel and another for a hammer, he succeeded in breaking a few inches off one side of the protruding wedge of sandstone. None of the younger boys who were small enough to squeeze through wanted to do it. An older boy with a very slim body said he would try. One end of a rope was tied around his waist and the other end was tied to a tree just outside the cave. It was a very tight fit but he squeezed past the sharp rock and went a few feet into the cave before he was heard to exclaim, "Oh, my god!" A lot of rope was quickly pulled into the cave. Then there was complete silence.

Gregg called to the boy several times but he didn't answer. The sun went behind a cloud and the woods got darker. A chilly wind started to blow up the hill. The noise of the wind through the trees made an eerie sound. Then a voice was heard from far inside the cave. "Hey, out there. You guys can stop worryin' now. Other than being a little wet and muddy, I'm O.K. Right now I'm at the bottom of a long narrow room that goes all the way across the inside of the hill. It's clean and empty like no one has ever been in here before. There are no signs of Indians or hidden treasure. You'll have to pull hard on the rope to help me get back up to the ledge at the entrance."

It took some serious tugging to get the boy back up to the entrance and out past the barrier rock. He was very glad to be the one who explored the secret cave on the hill. He was also glad to be safely outside again. He confessed he didn't answer right away because he thought it would be good fun to make everybody think something *mysterious* had happened. Because of the real danger of getting stuck or falling down from a ledge inside the cave, Gregg and boys closed the entrance with several big rocks. Then they covered the rocks with dirt and leaves. They knew it would be safer and they agreed it would be more fun to carry on the legend of the secret cave on the hill.

Gregg intuitively knew that the cave was there, even though the experts said it wasn't possible. He realized that this extraordinary cave probably was created when an ancient earthquake forced the hill to spread apart at its base and tip backward at the top to form a long narrow cavity. Sometime in the distant past erosion had uncovered an opening to this cavity with a large chunk of fractured rock sticking up in the middle. Such an opening, that invited curiosity to see what was inside and yet prevented anyone from entering, probably gave rise to the mystery stories that had been told about it over the years. In retrospect, Gregg realized that his discovery was not just happenstance. Like *knowing* that his teacher friend's train schedule had been changed without any ordinary communication to that effect, he *knew* that the cave was there. He was somehow able to tune in to information in the Universal Mind and visualize how it would be found.

Gregg eventually came to realize that his inexplicable *knowing* experiences were cases of pre-cognition. He had been able to pick up information from the Universal Mind and become aware of what he was going to experience before it actually happened. The information was out there. Somehow he had become "tuned" to the right frequency of vibrations from the Universal Mind that let him receive it. Just like the prophets. And the oracles. And the psychics. And the remote viewers that worked for the CIA during the Cold War years. In more superstitious times it was considered abnormal, even sacrilegious, for ordinary people to have such experiences. Now he realized that the ability to have such experiences was "no big deal." Lots of people have them. The ability to have them is among the innate capacities of all human beings. It can be developed with practice. Throughout history some people have always found themselves with this ability developed to a high level. Shamanic training, traumatic accidents, near death experiences, meditation, and major hormonal shifts are known to boost its development.

There was no doubt in his mind that having several of such experiences led him to learn about the Oracles of Delphi and to feel in his bones that some part of him had actually been a first-hand witness of this world renowned enterprise. In the summer of 1977 he had traveled through Greece with an international group of educators. Their itinerary included a special stop at Delphi. When he walked around the temple grounds on Mount Parnassus and looked out over the countryside below, he felt it was all strangely familiar. Each member of his travel group was instructed to select a short poem or passage that they felt was appropriate to the setting and be prepared to read it aloud from the amphitheater stage. Gregg chose a passage from *The Colossus of Maroussi*, by Henry Miller, that described an expansive and inclusive vision of the world inspired by the light of Greece. He read it passionately to the group, standing a few steps away from where the Oracles once sat in their swings suspended from copper and gold tripods. The tripods had then been placed over vents in the stone floor that conducted mildly intoxicating vapors from a fire-pit below. Gregg's audience sat on the ancient stone seats in the temple. While there were no vapors to assist him on that day, he was visibly moved and his reading was clearly inspired. He had come to Delphi after actually walking inside Agamemnon's beehive shaped tomb. What seemed like only an ancient myth, when he learned about it in History and World Literature classes, came powerfully alive as he entered the tomb excavation site. When he walked inside the massive underground structure and touched its walls of exquisitely crafted stones he felt he was slammed through a time warp to a new level of awareness. To find himself shortly thereafter where the Oracles lived and dispensed their wisdom was nearly overwhelming. When he read the following passage to his travel group, in the ruins of the temple at Delphi, he was truly transported.

> When I think of Katsimbalis bending over to pick a flower from the bare soil of Attica the whole Greek world, past, present, and future, rises before me. I see again the soft low mounds in which the illustrious dead were hidden away; I see the violet light in which the stiff scrub, the worn rocks, the huge boulders of the dry river beds gleam like mica; I see the miniature islands floating above the sea, ringed with dazzling white bands; I see the eagles swooping out from the dizzy crags of inaccessible mountaintops, their somber shadows slowly staining the bright carpet of earth below; I see the figures of solitary men trailing their flocks over the naked spine of the hills and the fleece of their beasts all golden fuzz as in the days of legend; I see the women gathered at the wells amidst the olive groves, their dress, their manners, their talk no different now than in Biblical times; I see the grand patriarchal figure of the priest, the perfect blend of male and female, his countenance serene, frank, full of peace and dignity; I see the geometrical pattern of nature expounded by the earth itself in a silence which is deafening. The Greek earth opens before me like the Book of Revelation. I never knew the earth contains so much; I had walked blindfolded, with faltering, hesitant steps; I was proud and arrogant, content to live the false, restricted life of the city man. The light of Greece opened my eyes, penetrated my pores, expanded my whole being. I came home to the world, having found the true center and real meaning of revolution. No warring conflicts between the nations of the earth can disturb this equilibrium. Greece herself may become embroiled, as we ourselves are now

becoming embroiled, but I refuse categorically to become anything less than the citizen of the world which I silently declared myself to be when I stood in Agamemnon's tomb. From that day forth my life was dedicated to the recovery of the divinity of man. Peace to all men, and life more abundant.

Like a smoldering coal in a fireplace, Gregg's experience at Delphi stayed alive in his mind and memory long after he returned home. If encouraged just a little it would come to brightness and stimulate a profusion of thought. Left alone it would quiet down to only glowing. It never died out. Many years later it became the subject of some powerful dreams that profoundly captured his attention and furthered his ability to communicate with the Universal Mind. In these dreams he was aware that some very important information was to be found in literature about the Oracles. The dreams became more frequent and more powerful. They were not frightening, only promising. So he went to the local library and looked for books about the Oracles of Delphi. He found nothing there. Consulting the interlibrary loan listings, he located only two books in the combined holdings of four major libraries. Both of these works drew upon legends and history recorded by other writers ranging from those who knew Delphi first hand, such as Homer and Plutarch, to contemporary explorers and archeologists who have tried to reconstruct the story of the Oracles. One of the books was so dull and unpromising that after skimming through it he decided it contained nothing worth the effort serious reading would require. He felt the other book was more interesting and might contain something of value, so he read it carefully from cover to cover. Again he found nothing unusual and began to doubt his dreams. He put the books in his car to take them back to the library the next day. That night he had another dream that encouraged him to go back to the second book. It was like a voice telling him he would find something important there if he would be alert and patient. When he picked up the book it almost fell open to a passage that he soon recognized as a revelation. The author stated that the Oracles of Delphi initially were girls about fifteen years old who had spontaneously exhibited pre-cognitive ability. Once identified as having this ability and a handsome appearance, the young women were brought to the Temple and placed in the care of the Temple Priests. The Priests acted as the business agents for the Oracle enterprise. They contracted with those who wanted answers to troubling questions, dispatched the women to consult the Universal Mind, and relayed their responses to the clients. They were also charged with keeping the women healthy and happy so they could do their best work.

Unfortunately, the temptation to take advantage of these attractive, talented, and dependent young women was too great in too many cases. Intimate involvement with their mentors disrupted their communication with the Universal Mind and diminished their precognitive accuracy. Later it was discovered that this ability was also manifest in females at about fifty years of age. When the accuracy of the younger women waned, they were replaced by older women who produced good results and were less difficult to maintain. Changing from young girls to fifty year old women propped up the Oracle enterprise for a time but the Priests' failure to properly care for their workers eventually put them out of business. Discovering how the world renowned Oracles lived and worked, Gregg was awakened to the fact that precognitive ability clearly is an inherent attribute that has been present in the various human populations and evolving for thousands of years.

Gregg understood that his dreams and discoveries about the Oracles were no coincidence. He knew he had been guided to the information so he could learn from it and use it to make better choices in his own life. It became clear to him that the temptation to exploit others for personal gain and gratification is an ever-present challenge. He recognized that the challenge might be met in negative and destructive ways or in ways that are positive and productive.

With that insight he also realized that positive and productive actions lead to a growing ability to experience loving relationships with other human beings. And, ultimately, that such actions would lead to connection with the source of all creation via the Universal Mind. He could see that human beings facing this challenge haven't always made the positive and productive choice. Whereas women with active pre-cognitive ability were recruited to serve as Oracles and treated with great reverence in Greek culture for a very long time, many in other situations were considered witches and drowned or burned at the stake. Sadly, prophets in all walks of life have paid a dear price for exhibiting their ability to access information from the Universal Mind. The changes required by such information were often seen as disruptive. They were threatening to those with vested interests and positions of power. The messengers were ridiculed, imprisoned, banned, or killed, to eliminate the perceived evil. "When that is taken into consideration," Gregg thought to himself, "it is a miracle that any new information from the Universal Mind has survived and gained acceptance."

Gregg was so intensely reviewing his memories that he barely noticed the pretty flight attendant who was asking him if he would like something to drink. He came alert briefly and mumbled, "Water, please." Then he went back into his memory bank. He felt that something important was happening as the memories came up and he moved into them. Like the order that is eventually created out of chaos, the spontaneous appearance of the scene and a tumult of associated feelings seemed to be coalescing into a meaningful pattern. He was fascinated and deeply wanted more.

After he drank the cup of water and the flight attendant had picked up the empty cup, he settled back into his seat and closed his eyes. Immediately, the memories started to bubble up again. He quickly remembered he was painfully aware that most of the beautiful stone columns of the temple at Delphi were missing when he visited there. He had asked what happened to them. No one seemed to know. A week later in Turkey he learned that Roman conquerors had pulled them down. Then they were hauled to the seacoast and loaded on ships that took them to Constantinople. There they were used in building the great Cathedral of Hagia Sophia. Later, Moslems captured the city of Constantinople and changed its name to Istanbul. The great Cathedral was altered to become a Mosque. Another revelation. One religious group after another had been conquered by force and their property used to build places of worship for a new order. Each group was certain they were the most worthy and had the best vision of God. Because they found the collective power to overcome others by force they felt invincible. They were certain their cause was right and God was on their side. Gregg shuddered at the realization of how much destruction, pain, and suffering had been wrought throughout history in the name of exclusive and excluding religious dogmas.

CHAPTER IV

Beyond Illusions

All Faith is false, all Faith is true:
Truth is the shattered mirror strown
in myriad bits; while each believes
his little bit the whole to own
                    ---Sir Richard Francs Burton

There was a lot of hustle in the aisles of the plane as passengers tried to get to the restrooms before food was served. Once the food carts were in a narrow aisle it was almost impossible to get by them for any reason. Gregg took advantage of the brief lull before the serving would start and made a trip to the rear of the plane. Sixth in line at the restrooms, he realized he didn't have much time before the food carts would be pushed out of the galley and block the only route back to his seat. He feared he would have to stand at the rear of the plane until the servers passed the row where his seat was located. He resented having to rush a process that should be done in gentle comfort and follow the dictates of nature. He suddenly remembered something he read a long time ago. The eminent Gestalt Psychologist, Fritz Perls, proposed that for good health there were two things people should take a long unhurried time to do: eating meals and taking a crap. When engaged in the latter that would mean no deadlines, no knocking at the door, and no cell phones. Every time he was forced to violate this wisdom, he felt that another little nick of damage was done to his mind and body. When it was his turn he went in and did what he could as quickly as possible. Washing his hands and responsibly cleaning the basin for the next user consumed a few more precious moments. He entered the aisle just a few seconds before the servers started to roll and quickly moved to his seat. There was some relief at doing something for his physical comfort and in winning the race with the servers. At the same time he felt he had not achieved complete satisfaction and probably had done himself a small amount of harm. He settled back in his seat and closed his eyes to meditate.

Before long the pleasant voice of the flight attendant again brought him back to alert awareness. He sat up and arranged his seatback table to receive a food tray. While he was glad to get some food, he realized that he would be imprisoned in his seat until the servers came back for the trays. With that in mind, he decided to follow Dr. Perls' advice and eat his food very slowly. He chewed everything more thoroughly than usual. He sipped his water slowly and rested a little between sips. He thought pleasant thoughts, especially of places and people he dearly loved. He had just finished the last bite of food and the last swallow of water when the servers came back for his tray. He felt comfortable, at last, and ready for a nap. However, when he closed his eyes another potent memory that had been filed away for many years came flashing up. He was a senior at the College of Education in the State University at Rockton. It would soon be time to look for a job. The College Placement Bureau had met with the seniors and instructed them to prepare a Candidate's Statement to include in their placement records. This usually meant the candidate would write several pages in which they would describe their achievements and project how they could contribute to a school system that hired them. Gregg tried to do what was expected. After several unsatisfactory efforts he knew he had to do something different and outside the norm. He wanted his statement to help him find a certain type of prospective employer at the same time it presented his best attributes for a teaching job. His intuition strongly guided him to write the following brief Candidate's Statement:

I believe that what I get out of anything is directly
proportionate to what I put into it. I try to see the world
and things in a general focus, not judging by the moment
or isolated incident. Emotional maturity is, to me, the
greatest goal in this life and can only be reached through
a life of productivity and an awareness of the truth. I try
to practice basic honesty with myself and with others as
I hold it a prerequisite to real happiness that I believe can
only be spiritual. I do not want a routine job, but rather one
in which I can assist things to grow.

Gregg reasoned that an employer who understood and saw the
value of this statement would be someone he would like to work
for. Those who didn't understand or like it he would be glad to
have eliminated from consideration. Shortly after submitting it, he
was summoned to a conference with the Placement Director. She
gruffly told him that his Statement was inadequate for a graduate
of the College of Education and would cause him serious problems
in the job market. She strongly advised him not to have it put in
his Placement Records. When he explained why he thought this
statement was best for him and asked that it be kept in his file, she
was unable to conceal her feeling that this was a very bad move.

As other candidates had favorable interviews and departed for
their new jobs, he began to feel like the kid who is left standing while
all of the others are chosen to be on a team. Not one prospective
employer invited him to be interviewed. He suspected that the
Placement Director was so set against his Candidate's Statement that
she probably did what she could to keep it out of sight. At the same
time he was glad not to be going to work in any of the job situations
that had been listed at the Placement Bureau. His intuition told him
that everything would work out to his benefit if he would be patient
and pay attention.

Gregg's handling of the matter certainly resulted from long use of
creative resources to survive in a hostile environment. Of necessity,

he had learned to see and act upon new possibilities. They almost always seemed safer and friendlier than the usual way of doing things. Conforming was restrictive and sometimes dangerous. Creating was fun. He had gone to the university with these characteristics and attitudes. The atmosphere in his classes was generally tolerant and accepting. At least it was after he got past the entry gatekeepers who gave him a battery of achievement and aptitude tests. After the tests were scored, they hauled him in and roughly demanded to know how he had cheated. They said that coming from a poor small-town high school it wasn't possible for him to make the high scores he did without cheating. He was made to take several of the tests over again under intense supervision. When he scored even better under these conditions, they were still skeptical. They were sure there had to be a trick involved somehow. However, they offered a measured apology and admitted him on probation.

In large lecture classes he got along fairly well. He soon learned not to ask too many questions. Just listen, take notes and study so he could give it back the way the professor liked it. In some smaller classes, he was more visible and experienced some conflict. Especially in math. One professor even resorted to the kind of ridicule he thought he left behind in Sand Creek. As this professor was passing back some quiz papers in class one day, he stopped at Gregg's desk. Holding Gregg's paper up for all to see, he said loudly, "This is some of the most ridiculous work I have ever seen. Your answers are right but your calculations don't follow any correct procedures. It seems like you used intuition more than understanding." And he laughed. Gregg was mortified and angry. He thought about hanging the professor by his thumbs from the street lamp he could see through a side window.

After class a pretty girl came up to him and let it be known that she thought the math professor was a jerk. They talked for several minutes and then she suggested they go to the Campus Union for something to eat. More friendly talk. About school, basketball (very big in Indiana), where to go off-campus for fun, and more about the math class. Eventually, she offered to help him with the math if he would help her with the physics labs. He was doing quite well with the lab work and saw this as a fair trade. What he didn't know was that other students in the physics labs had observed him at work there. They saw the instructor respond favorably to his questions and give approval for his efforts. This information had been reported back to the sorority house and his "math helper" had been assigned to gain access to his lab reports for the sorority house files. One day she asked if she could take his lab reports with her to study at the library and return them to him at the Union later in the afternoon. He agreed and went to the Union at the appointed time. She didn't show. He tried calling her at the number she gave him. A female voice told him she wasn't there. After four calls and waiting for over an hour, he reluctantly went home. He was puzzled and panicked. His reports were due in lab class the next afternoon.

When he approached his math class the next morning, she was waiting on the steps outside the building. She apologized for not showing up the day before. She claimed she was ill and was worried that he would think that the lab reports were lost. She handed them to him and he stowed them away in his book bag. He had started to like her and said that he was really sorry she wasn't feeling well. She blushed and said, "let's go into class. It's the last one before the final exam. Meet me out here afterward. I have something important to tell you."

After class she was waiting on the steps with a sad look on her face. She told him that she felt terrible about what she had done. She said she enjoyed helping him with his math and talking with him over food at the Union. Then she confessed that she didn't show up the day before because she and some of her sorority sisters were copying his lab reports for the house files. She said, "If there's any good to come from this deception, your papers are going to help a lot of girls get through physics lab. Why you? You were chosen because you really seemed to understand that stuff. It's really hard for a lot of people. I'm really sorry. You are a nice guy and I don't think you deserve this kind of treatment." As she turned and walked away he felt an overwhelming sense of loss. He saw himself as naïve. Unsophisticated. Easily deceived. A babe not completely out of the woods. Rejected one more painful time. He wasn't sure which hurt more, being abused or being used. On the other hand, his lab reports had been the object of her deception because they were very good. He spontaneously started humming a line from the song that the *Little Rascal* Alfalfa always sang to Darla, "The object of my affection (substitute deception) can turn my complexion from white to rosy red," and then he began to chuckle. He decided that anything anyone else could learn, he could learn it too. And he would survive in this university no matter what.

His classes went fairly well after he recovered from his election to the sorority hall of fame. Until he met up with the professor who taught a required course widely known as "bean bags." The catalog title of the course was *The Theory and Practice of Play.* It was supposed to prepare prospective teachers for safe, fun, and educational things to do with children at play times. In fact, it was mostly library research and writing note cards. Developing a file of note cards with one game or activity to a card. Twenty cards each week. If you were late turning in your cards, the number was doubled for each day you were overdue. Even if you were sick. No excuses were accepted. The tyranny of this arbitrary and unreasonable situation spawned an active commerce in illicit game cards. Some trading. Some purchasing. Some bargaining by desperate individuals to get others to turn in their quota of cards for them when they couldn't make it to class. But no matter what the students did, nobody ever got an A for the course.

The tyrannical professor had come to the conclusion that the ultimate toy for playing games with children was the beanbag. In every class he would demonstrate its many uses and extol its superior qualities. He was so enamored of this safe, inexpensive, and versatile toy that he routinely offered an automatic A for the entire course to any student that brought him a waterproof filler with all the other attributes of beans. Many students tried. Just as many failed. The professor delighted in checking them out by the criteria he had developed from the attributes of natural beans. When the offer of an automatic A was made to Gregg's class, he immediately started to think *outside the box (or in this case the bag).* He knew he could beat the professor at his own game. He knew he could find a substitute for the beans that had all of their good characteristics and would not be ruined when they got wet.

And he did. For several afternoons he went to a leather shop in Sand Creek where he used a hammer and an old leather punch to pound out bean-shaped pieces of rubber from discarded inner tubes for truck tires. When he had enough, he sewed them into a denim bag just like the professor's favorite model. He was excited when he took it to class. Partly because he knew his creation would do the job. Even more because he knew he would dumbfound the professor who got so much pleasure out of tearing students' creations apart. At the beginning of each class, anyone who had a "possible" was invited to toss it up to the professor and then play with him while he took the bag through its paces. Gregg was the last to toss his bag into play. Eight others had seen theirs go down for the count. The professor gave a pinched and funny smile when he felt Gregg's special creation in his hand. When it passed all of the tests he accused Gregg of trying to play a joke on him by using real beans. He ripped open the bag to expose the fraud in front of the class. When the rubber pellets tumbled out, it was obvious to everyone that they even went one better than natural beans because they were impervious to water. He was speechless. Everyone knew that Gregg had achieved the automatic A. So he stopped writing the hated note cards. His grade was secure because he met the challenge and he had witnesses, right? Wrong! He had witnesses, OK. And they were singing his praises. But, like Yogi Berra once said, "It's not over 'til it's over." And it wasn't. When the grades were posted, there was a B instead of an A for Gregg. As the other students in the class learned that the professor had reneged on his long standing commitment they were enraged. They wanted Gregg to go over to the professor's house and demand that he change the grade. A large group of supporters volunteered to go with him. He quickly agreed, and the march was on. But when the angry entourage got to the professor's house they were told by one of his neighbors that he had left early that morning for a long vacation. He simply couldn't ruin his reputation by giving an A in his course, even if it meant going back on his word. And there was no way he could face the student whose creative ingenuity he felt might require him to compromise his pedagogical principles. So, he skipped town immediately after posting his usual preconceived and arbitrary grades. Another teacher who was stuck with his own limited illusion and unable to appreciate Gregg's ability to see outside of it.

Connecting with a mentor who nurtured exceptional talents

With the bitter effects of the "bean bags" experience still in his mind, he entered another required education course. That's when he met Maxine. Talk about synchronicity, this meeting at this time was surely a guided event. Maxine taught courses that focused on how to help children learn. She was a passionate believer in "learning by doing." The kind of "hands on" learning described by psychologist John Dewey in his seminal book *Democracy and Education (1916)* and reformulated two decades later in *Experience and Education (1938)*. She didn't just believe it and talk about it in the courses she taught, she was able to "practice what she preached." The experience Gregg had with Maxine not only supported and utilized his creative abilities, it taught him how to do the same for others.

During the introduction to her social studies *methods* course, Maxine encouraged the participants to discuss the strengths and weaknesses of their own education up to that point. It was soon apparent that most of their experience had been focused on listening, reading, memorizing, and taking tests. Often with arbitrary and poorly prepared teachers who were more concerned with classroom control than helping students to learn. While the infamous "bean bags" course was considered extreme and got plenty of air time in passionate discussion, there were many other "war stories" to share. Much had been repressed and accepted as *just the way it was.* They vowed that they would not do those things to their own future students. Maxine summarized their discussions and then cited some disturbing research findings that showed most teachers had a tendency to teach as they were taught. Under stress, they would automatically revert to what they had learned at the hands of their parents and teachers. Doing anything else was very difficult because their view of what a classroom was like was limited to what they had experienced. Most of them had never seen a teacher work in any other way. She also said that what they had experienced, and worse, was still going on in schools, "even in these enlightened times and within a few miles of this great university." Her remarks set Gregg's imagination into high gear. He decided he would go out there and check this out for himself.

One day, while driving and searching on some country roads near the university, he hit pay dirt. About 25 miles from the campus, he discovered a one-room school with outdoor toilets and no electricity. After securing permission from the County Superintendent of Schools, he contacted the teacher and arranged to visit the school. When he arrived at the school in the early afternoon, the sky was overcast. He was introduced to the students and invited to sit at a table in the back of the room. Sitting there in the dim light that came only from the windows, he found himself getting depressed. It was obvious that the teacher and the students at the front of the room near the single wood stove were plenty warm. Back where he was sitting it was definitely cooler. The fifth graders got ready to "recite" their health lesson. This consisted of taking turns reading aloud from their health books. The lesson that day was about the best kind of lighting to protect their eyes while reading. He found the irony of this situation almost overwhelming. He decided to write about what he had seen and share it with Maxine. At the end of the school day, he thanked everyone for allowing him to visit and spent some time talking with the friendly students on the playground. Strongly moved by the inequities he had witnessed, he went home and wrote a poignant account of his impressions. He took it to Maxine at her office. She invited him to have a seat while she read it. He wanted her to know what he had discovered and that what she had said in class inspired him to make the search. At the same time, he was afraid she might think he was being a nuisance. When she finished reading, the smile on her face made it clear that she was pleased with his efforts. She asked if he would be willing to read it aloud to the class the next day. He was surprised. And relieved. And pleased! Before he remembered how vulnerable he felt in front of a group, he agreed to do it.

Maxine didn't see Gregg's creative energy as a problem and seek ways to shut him down. She was delighted at his efforts and thought a lot about how to encourage him. She knew she could respond to what he had written in ways that would set in motion a real "learning by doing" experience for everyone in the course. The next day she reminded the group of her previous remarks and described what Gregg had done. Then she asked him to read his paper. When he finished, there was dead quiet. Nobody moved or spoke. He wondered if he had made a big mistake. Did they think he was "on the stage" wasting class time when they had important stuff to learn? Maxine waited patiently. Then someone spoke up. Their voice cracked a little. It was clear that they were deeply moved. Others soon joined in. Their contributions were animated. Maxine facilitated their discussion, summarizing their ideas and putting them on the chalkboard. At the peak of their compassionate interest in this little school and its inhabitants, she offered them a challenge: *Adopt this school as a class project and learn about improving a school situation by actually doing things to make it better.* She told them class time could be used for planning sessions, reporting progress, trouble shooting problems, and meeting with invited guests who might be of assistance. She also said that their grade in the course could be based on their participation, a term paper describing what they learned, and their own self-evaluation. The choice was made by secret ballot. It was unanimous. If the superintendent and the teacher agreed, they would do their best to make that school a better place for educating kids. The rest of the class that day was given over to thinking about how to get approval from the Superintendent and the teacher. Maxine asked questions, offered suggestions, summarized their contributions, and generally kept things moving. Gregg and two other students were delegated to meet with the superintendent, share their proposal, and seek his approval. They reported back to the class that he not only approved of their proposal, he volunteered to come to the university and discuss the situation with their class. In a lively give and take discussion a week later, the visiting superintendent reiterated something Maxine also had told them on the first day of class. *Teachers have a tendency to teach as they were taught and it was very difficult to see any other ways of doing things.* He said the teacher at the school they would be working on was a kind and cooperative person with a limited view of how to make improvements in her teaching. She had told him she would welcome their help and some fresh ideas. So the project was sanctioned by the local power structure and Maxine's students were off and running. The enthusiasm was so high that somebody joked they now knew how Mighty Mouse must have felt when he swooped in to *save the day!*

It turned out that *saving the day* was a lot more complex than anyone dreamed it would be. Small groups of students took turns going out to the school, until everyone had made a visit. They timed their visits so they could observe classroom activities and be on the playground with the students during recess or after lunch. After each visit they made notes to share with their classmates back on campus. From discussions of these notes, specific needs of the school were identified. The list was enormous. By now Maxine had relinquished her place at the chalkboard to two speedwriters. They worked furiously to list every contribution. When all of the ideas were listed, they discussed each of them and placed it in a category according to content. Work groups were then formed for each category. A steering committee was also formed, with one member from each work group, to set up a master schedule and keep everyone informed. And so the work began.

What they accomplished was nothing short of miraculous. The library group asked everyone in the class to go through all of their books at home and bring in any they were willing to contribute. The group then categorized the books according to grade level and created a substantial reading library for he school. The utilities group discovered that a rural electric power line had recently been installed to serve a farmhouse near the school. They located an electrician who agreed to supply materials at cost and supervise the members while they helped him prepare the school for its first electric lights. Three groups decided to organize a meeting with the children's parents to explain what they were trying to do and to solicit their help. The positive response far exceeded their expectations. Paint was donated and a weekend painting session was planned. Several parents showed up to help the enthusiastic future teachers paint the interior walls of the building a light and pleasant color. The old blackboards were sanded smooth and then given a fresh coat of non-glare green chalkboard paint. Two evening sessions were organized for removing the old desks from the floor and placing them on short wooden runners so they could be moved around for small group activities. One Saturday morning a group met with some parents who brought power tools and weather proofed boards and helped them rebuild the front porch. The school bus driver brought an army surplus heavy equipment jack and it was used to take most of the sag out of the main beam under the floor. Some other parents brought used cement blocks and closed the gaps between the stone support pillars to keep out disturbing animals and icy winds. The physical education and playground group asked everyone to bring in any old games and/or sports equipment they might find at home that the owners would be willing to give to the school. They took the resulting supply of games and equipment out to the school and stayed for recess or after lunch on several occasions to organize games and teach skills. They also had responsibility for improving one situation for which their best idea came from one of the young students at the school. The outdoor toilets were very drafty and cold in the winter. The student's idea was similar to one his folks had implemented at their farm. Line the inside of the toilets with cardboard. Put a lighted farm lantern inside during the school day. Store it in the schoolhouse at other times. The group members quickly saw the value of this idea. To put it operation at the school they went to some appliance stores near the university and acquired several refrigerator boxes that were destined for the trash heap. One Saturday morning they went out to the school to line the inside walls of the toilets with cardboard panels they cut from the discarded boxes. Several students who lived close enough to the school to walk or ride their bikes showed up and asked if they could help. They were allowed to take turns using staple guns to fasten the cardboard snugly to the walls. When the job was done, the members of the project group stayed awhile to play some games with the kids. As they were leaving, the kids thanked them for the great improvement to the toilets and for teaching them the games.

Maxine was always available in class or in her office. She was both catalyst and facilitator. She went out to the school and worked alongside the students. She was there when they met with parents at perhaps the only such meeting that ever had been held at the school. She was a live and wise resource person. She gave the members of her class *freedom from* arbitrary and irrational restrictions. That, alone, could have amounted to abandonment. However, through questions, guidance, suggestions, feedback, obliging them to analyze results of their efforts, and directing them to relevant research findings at appropriate times, she also gave them *freedom to* be creative and learn from their own experience. When she helped them to examine their total experience critically during the last week of the course, she drew their attention to the limits of people's illusions. She emphasized how difficult it was to see outside of those illusions to find new and better ways of doing things. She said they had broken through the perception barrier; and the process they used was one that they could emloy over and over again. She told them that half of the information available at the time would be obsolete in ten years. Also, that half of what they would need to know in ten years hadn't been developed yet. The *process* they used would always be effective. Gregg thrived in the kind of educational environment she provided. From that day forward, he employed the *process* Maxine helped him learn about and creatively apply in different situations. He knew the power of this approach that he had "learned by doing" with the guidance of a wise and caring facilitator.

Finding a universal way to use special attributes and abilities

Gregg had always found ways to see outside the prevailing illusions. When he was younger he climbed small trees on the wooded hills around the town of Sand Creek where he could sway and sing. A little later he built spectacular tree houses. His best was in a great sycamore tree that leaned at an angle of about forty-five degrees out over the creek as it meandered between the hills south of town. It had a built-in bunk bed where he could lay and read a book while fishing out of the window. It was a place he dearly loved. The creek was about a mile south of town. The tree house overlooked a deep pool at a big shady bend in the creek. There was a high wooded bluff on the east side. A fringe of trees and undergrowth between the water's edge and abandoned farm pasture sloped gently up from the west side. Hidden from view unless you were up close. A huge field of wild bluebells at the base of the giant and friendly sycamore tree. Safety. Peace. Deep tranquility. Only the sounds of the woodlands and the flow of water over the shallow riffle a few yards downstream. A sanctuary almost as good as the trees he climbed on the north side of town to sway back and forth above it all while he sang his troubles away. He was able to enjoy the fruits of his creative labor for several weeks without being discovered. However, one day some bigger boys noticed that he was often coming home from somewhere down the creek with a stringer full of fish. They decided to wait for his next trip and follow him to find out where he was being so lucky. When they succeeded in their sneaky efforts and saw his magnificent tree house, they felt they had struck gold. They scurried up the big sycamore tree and captured him. They broke his fishing poles, cursed him, and roughed him up a little. They told him to never come back there again because they were taking over the tree house. Then they threw him in the creek and the biggest boy said, "swim to the other side you little bastard and get the hell out of here." He quickly did as he was told.

Scrambling toward town along the foot of the bluff, he vowed they would not get away with their thievery. A week later, on a Sunday morning when those "good" boys had gone to church with their folks, he went back to the sycamore tree with a wrecking bar and a can of kerosene. He completely dismantled the tree house. Then he piled the boards in a heap, soaked them with kerosene, and set them on fire. When the conquerors returned to the scene for an afternoon of fishing and fun, all they found was the charred and smoking remains. They were sadly disappointed and vowed to "get that little son-of-a-bitch." Gregg was sad too. Not for what he had done to spoil their fun. Just for the loss of his handiwork. The special tree house he had built with his own two hands and ingenuity. A place where he could be by himself and think about what was happening in his life.

Reflecting on his tree house situation and such challenges that were often thrust upon him while he was growing up in Sand Creek, Gregg came to a disturbing realization. Until he met Maxine his creative energies had been expended mostly in defending himself, showing off, or learning in isolation. His experience with her inclusive attitude and "learning by doing" methods showed him how to transcend the negatives of those experiences and become an effective change agent in the real world. His orientation to the world and his place in it was profoundly altered. He was increasingly able to use the methods she helped him learn to make creative and useful contributions wherever he found himself.

Ironically, his first teaching job was in his old hometown of Sand Creek! He learned that the small and impoverished school system there was in desperate need of teachers. When he applied for a teaching position the interviewing clerk didn't ask many questions or make any demands. His candidate's statement didn't help him get the job or stand in his way. It simply didn't matter to his employers who just wanted a certified body to fill the position. The salary offered was among the lowest in the state. There was little or no money for teaching equipment and materials. The situation would have presented a daunting challenge to most new teachers but he was actually pleased. Under these conditions he would have the freedom to do things his way. The old two-story brick schoolhouse served about three hundred students in grades one through twelve. He was assigned to teach grade six in a classroom on the first floor. It had many features that were similar to the country school his *methods* class had adopted. Mostly in what was lacking. Books. Equipment. Supplies. Even permanent records for the students. All things that he found ways to provide by using the *process* he learned in his work with Maxine.

Processing positive changes in a dysfunctional environment

The "learning by doing" that took place that year included many powerful experiences, in and out of the classroom, for both his students and himself. During one animated discussion on how to make learning the required subjects more fun and useful, his students figured out how to equip their classroom for active learning. Get parents to loan tools and machines (a jigsaw, a lathe, handsaws, chisels, planes, etc.). Rewrite instructions for making lamps, birdhouses, gun racks, and other craft projects, to use the math concepts they were supposed to learn. Set up study groups where those who knew the math would help those who didn't. Have testing to find out when students were ready for working in the "shop." A retired building contractor heard about what they were doing and offered to buy the materials and draw the plans to build three work tables for their shop, if Gregg would promise to have the students do the building.

They learned how the Romans moved heavy objects with leveraged manpower by cutting donated trees on a wooded hill outside of town and carrying the logs back to the school. They found it easy to do when smaller poles were tied across each log and 6 boys and girls positioned themselves along the cross poles and lifted in unison when a command was given. In this manner they carried 4 logs, each about 5 inches in diameter and 12 feet long, 2 miles into town for use in building a backstop for their softball field. Originally this field was a farm pasture adjacent to the school grounds. It had a small hill in the middle that was too high for right fielders to see the batter. They had to watch for signals from the center fielder up on the hill and then scan the sky. A class meeting was held to discuss how to manage this situation better. One student volunteered that his uncle drove a big earthmover for the county highway department that could easily level the field. A delegation including this boy went to meet with his uncle and one evening, after a normal workday, the hill was removed. The earth was redistributed to make a level playing field. Two other boys, whose family farm was close by, arranged for Gregg to drive their farm tractor with a disc attached for a couple of evenings to work the surface of the field into fine particles so grass could be planted. Another group went to a school board meeting with Gregg to present what had been done and ask for a truckload of lime dust to neutralize the exposed yellow clay so grass would grow. They were warmly received and the purchase was approved. After school one day several students went with Gregg to a nearby sawmill for sawdust to fill burlap feed bags and make bases for their ball field. Using borrowed tools and ropes the students dug holes for their backstop logs and hoisted them into place. Next, they stapled donated chicken wire (fencing) to the poles to complete an elegant softball field. Finally, they worked out a schedule with the other classes so that all of the students in the school had access to the field at a designated time.

They did some fascinating things to make their study of the Roman Empire, a major topic in their social studies textbook, more active and fun. They sold garden seeds and salt water taffy to raise money for a bus trip to Indianapolis to see the great Roman Epic: *Quo Vadis.* They held a Roman banquet in their classroom while wearing togas and long flowing chitons made of bed sheets. They drew lots for the roles they would play: nobles, slaves, entertainers, and beautiful maidens who peeled grapes for the reclining diners. They did research on the kinds of foods that were served at such banquets and got their mothers to help them prepare things to bring for their simulation of life in Roman times.

Gregg arranged with former professors and their colleagues at the university in Rockton to have graduate students in guidance and counseling do the first ever diagnostic testing of his students. Parents provided the funds to charter a bus for "a day at the university." However, he soon realized he went too far in selling the testing to one of his students. The boy had been "hard of hearing" since he entered first grade. He had always been assigned a front row seat so he could hear better. He was reluctant to have his hearing tested until Gregg told him that if he qualified for a hearing aids he could become the best squirrel hunter in the county. To drive the point home he said, "You can go out in the woods and turn up the volume and hear the squirrels breathing in their nests." When the results of the hearing test showed that his hearing loss was 100% correctable with medication, the student was crushed. No hearing aids were prescribed. He really wanted them and felt he had been tricked. It was a serious lesson for Gregg: not to promise more than might be delivered. Especially to kids.

The list of things accomplished by these students with their learning by doing activities was enormous. They were extremely energized with team spirit. He mused that when the power of youth is released in creative and productive ways the results are often far beyond normal expectations of what kids can do. Their softball team had such faith in what they could accomplish that they handily won games with bigger and older kids. They made spectacular and impossible plays that thrilled their parents and other onlookers. They also put on a gymnastics show for the public that included extraordinary rope climbing and tumbling feats. The President of the local PTA was so impressed that she sent them a letter of commendation and a check for $50.00 (of her own money) to buy something for their classroom. With these and many other unusual activities that made his students *enthusiastic* to go to school and learn, he soon established himself as a gifted teacher.

At the same time, his use of the *methods* he learned in Maxine's class went far beyond his students and their exceptional learning activities. He organized the first teachers' professional organization in the county and was elected its president for the next three years. He also mobilized parents, teachers, and other community volunteers to add three badly needed classrooms and a cafeteria to the overcrowded school. Most of the materials and all of the labor were donated. A wide variety of fundraisers provided the money to buy supplies not available through donations. They worked evenings and weekends throughout the summer. When the work was completed they held a joyful carnival on the school grounds to celebrate. While this job didn't pay much it offered two important features he had identified in his "rejected" candidate's statement. It certainly wasn't routine. And there were plenty of opportunities to "assist things to grow." The range of his personal awareness was also growing at a rapid pace.

Choosing to go forth and grow

News of Gregg's accomplishments got around and eventually brought him an offer to teach general science at one of the country's best school systems in an upscale suburb of Chicago. He took the job and worked there happily for several years. When he made this move he continued to follow in Maxine's footsteps. He brought his learning by doing approach to a situation that was traditionally focused on reading a textbook, watching teacher demonstrations, sometimes watching an educational film, and taking written tests. There were tense moments at first, until the students understood how he wanted to teach them. After working through the conflicts in their teaching and learning expectations, they expanded their educational environment to the entire metropolitan area. They learned the basics through lab exercises, demonstrations, reading research, and watching a wide variety of audiovisual presentations. Then they went on field trips to learn first-hand how this information was manifest in the world around them. They visited factories, museums, university laboratories, and water filtration plants. They even went digging for fossils in glacial deposits and stone quarries on all day trips downstate with expert consultants from the Illinois Geological Survey. They went on scavenger hunts for evidence of science principles in grocery and hardware stores. Moreover, they were involved in the planning and arrangements for these special experiences. Committees were elected to explore possible field trip sites. These committees went with Gregg to assess whether a proposed trip could be a worthwhile learning experience. If their findings were positive, the committee members then reported back to their classes and instructed them on all aspects of the trip. They made maps of the facilities that located restrooms, lunch areas, hazards (if any) to watch for, and where the bus would park for departure. They prepared instruction sheets that included study questions, time schedules, meeting locations, and what to do in case of an emergency. They also recruited parents to serve as emergency resource persons on the trip. In short, they were involved in the *process* of creating effective learning situations for themselves. The students' initial lethargy and resistance were soon replaced with genuine enthusiasm. When Gregg became President of the Chicago Area Teachers Science Association, several of the original "foot draggers" actually volunteered to participate in the annual science fairs this organization sponsored at the Field Museum in Chicago. Many more of them developed projects for exhibition in the fairs. Others did most of the background work to set up the fair and assist student exhibitors. They even typed the certificates and prepared the ribbons. Gregg had to watch them closely to see that they took time out for lunch. He was amazed at their motivation and excellent contributions when they saw that someone truly believed in them.

Mixing intuition and intention to effect a healing

During his third year of teaching junior high school science Gregg was presented with the opportunity to use Aunt Mamie's *gift*. A boy in one of his seventh grade classes had a very bothersome wart on his right hand. It was located where it was often bumped or scraped in the course of his everyday activities. Disturbance to the point of bleeding was common. The boy detested the wart and had tried various home remedies to remove it. None of them had worked. Peter and his family had emigrated from Germany to the United States. He was small for his age and spoke with a slight but noticeable accent. He was very personable and friendly. For many years his family had affectionately called him Fritz. He liked that name and encouraged everyone to make it his name at school. He loved tricks and jokes. He had a special thing that he could do and no one else could duplicate. He could make both of his eyes vibrate like Mexican jumping beans. He was good fun to have around. He often came in after the last class period to help Gregg clean lab equipment and prepare for the next day. He and Gregg became the best of friends. He invested a lot of trust in Gregg and his methods as *a man of science*. That set the stage for a special healing experience that drew upon the *gift*.

Gregg observed that Fritz experienced his wart as an extreme nuisance. He had to wear rubber gloves when washing beakers and test tubes for science labs. He carried a pocketful of Band-Aids to be ready for the frequent minor injuries that drew blood and negative comments from his peers. Other kids didn't want to hold hands with him in gym classes or during playground games. One afternoon when they were about to finish preparations for the next day's labs he looked up at Gregg with pleading (and non-vibrating) eyes and said, "Couldn't you do something to help me get rid of this wart?" His earnest request made Gregg want to help him if he could. He said, "There is something we might try. I'll check into it and see if I have the right stuff on hand or if I'll have to get some more. I'll let you know." Fritz put on a big grin and set his eyes to vibrating. It was a definite sign that he firmly believed his science teacher hero was going to do something scientific to make the wart go away.

Something that Gregg had once read in a journal came bounding into his awareness. The article was about curing warts. The doctor who did the study found that all manner of cures worked *if the person doing the treatment believed in it.* It didn't matter whether the person receiving the treatment believed in it or even if they knew they were being treated. As he pondered that information, he suddenly connected it with something in a film he had recently shown to some of his classes. The film was about tadpoles. How they developed from eggs and had tails they used for swimming. The narrator of the film had made a very curious remark. "Contrary to common belief, the tail does not drop off when the tadpole matures into a frog. It is absorbed into its body." He thought to himself, "If a tadpole can absorb a whole tail into its body, why can't a human body absorb a wart? And if I *believe* that's possible when I *treat* the wart that Fritz wants me to remove from his hand, it should work." With this information drawn from scientific studies to back up his *gift* from Aunt Mamie, he developed a treatment plan for Fritz. In the science room storage cabinets he located a large brown bottle that appeared ominously scientific. He washed and rewashed the bottle several times until it was squeaky-clean. He then partially filled it with distilled water. He did the same with an ugly old syringe. The treatment plot was set.

When Fritz came into class the next day, Gregg told him to come around after the last period so they could talk about removing his wart. Fritz vibrated his eyes furiously to signal his happy anticipation. When he returned later that afternoon, Gregg told him to pay close attention as he described the procedure they might use before school the next morning. He then showed him the bottle and syringe.

"If you are willing to go through with this, I'd like to practice how we'll do it a couple of times just so we get it exactly right. OK?"

"Sure," he said (with his eyes vibrating).

"Stand over here by the sink. I want you to be right next to the faucet. I have some very powerful stuff in this bottle that will get rid of your wart for sure. But I don't want you to end up with a big hole in your hand instead of a wart so it is very important for you to count to ten and then get your hand under the running water immediately. We'll just use some tap water instead of the chemical while we're practicing. OK?"

"OK," he said (with his eyes held steady).

"Put your hand right here over the sink. You'll have to hold it steady while I put five drops of the chemical on your wart. When you hear me say five, you start counting to ten in a normal voice. Then you immediately turn on the faucet and flush the stuff off your hand. If you get *any* of the chemical splashed on you, on your face or your other hand, even a drop, stick your hand or your face under the faucet immediately and let the water run for awhile. Ready to practice?"

"Yeah," he said (with his eyes vibrating). Let's do it."

Gregg maintained a very serious demeanor while they practiced several times until Fritz got it just right. He then locked the bottle and syringe back in the storage cabinet. At the appointed time next morning, Fritz showed up brimming with enthusiasm. He got in position by the sink, vibrated his eyes, and said he was ready. Gregg unlocked the cabinet. He brought the bottle and syringe to the table by the sink. He carefully filled the syringe and wiped the tip so there were no stray drops to cause a problem. Then the operation was performed with great seriousness and (exaggerated) concern for safety.

"Now, this stuff is already working on your wart. Just forget about it and the thing will be completely gone in a few days. It should be gone by Tuesday or Wednesday of next week."

"Will it drop off? Will I be able to find it? You want me to bring it in for a specimen?"

"No, it won't drop off in one piece. I doubt if you'll be able to find much of anything. Just be happy that you won't have to put up with it anymore."

"OK. You want me to help you clean up and put this stuff away?"

"No, thanks. I'll take care of it (as he obviously puts on rubber gloves). There really isn't that much to do. Have a good weekend. I'll see you on Monday."

"Yeah. OK. Thanks for helping me. I really appreciate it."

After Fritz left the room Gregg put the treatment tools back in the storage cabinet. He smiled to himself as he thought of what had taken place. The boy's eager and trusting face. The power he could feel transferring from himself to Fritz. The *knowing* that wart would soon be gone. The buzz that Fritz would create around the school when he discovered he was *cured*. What this feat would do for his (Gregg's) standing with all of the other students. Wondering what Aunt Mamie would think of his backing up the *gift* with some theatrics and a little science.

When Fritz woke up on Tuesday morning, his wart was gone! The skin where it used to be was smooth and unblemished. He was very excited and happy. He ran downstairs to show his parents. His older sister heard the loud talk and sleepily stumbled in to see what was going on. Fritz showed her the clean smooth skin on his hand where the hated growth used to be. She joined him in laughing and dancing around the kitchen to celebrate the *cure*. On his way to school he told several classmates about it and showed them his hand. By the time he got to the front door, he was leading an entourage of kids like the Pied Piper. He stopped to explain to a couple of curious teachers why everyone was so excited. By lunchtime everybody at the school knew what had happened. Gregg and Fritz were minor celebrities for the next few days. For Gregg, being the focus of such attention was a lot more than he wanted. However, Fritz loved it. His sister later came up to Gregg in a local grocery store to tell him he was a real hero to her brother. "He talks about you all the time and he *believes* whatever you say. He is always telling us Mr. Emerson said this and Mr. Emerson said that. When you fixed his wart, you got him completely."

Many years passed before Gregg understood what happened to make that wart disappear. He thought it must have been absorbed like the tadpoles absorb their tales. He strongly wanted that to happen. He somehow *knew* that it would. But he wasn't sure how the absorbing process was activated. What the *power* was in Aunt Mamie's *gift* that changed the living cells of a human body. Why it worked with people and animals that were not even aware of being treated. Why the common factor in successful treatment was the positive belief and directed thinking of the healer.

In recent times, he learned that the mystery has been unraveled by a number of scientific investigations, including carefully controlled double-blind studies. It has been firmly established that human thought can effect changes in human and animal tissue. It can also effect changes in plants. And it can do this over long distances. Intentional thought is the key. The healing effects of prayer and other forms of intentional thought are well documented in *Be Careful What you Pray For,* by Larry Dossey, M.D. Likewise in *Miracles of Mind* by Russell Targ and Jane Katra, Ph.D. These authors have drawn together a wealth of information obtained from the Universal Mind by many people around the world through intuition, personal experience, and careful research. This information suggests that the ability to use intentional thought for healing purposes is a latent attribute of all human beings. Like the ability to sing, to dance, or to play musical instruments, it may appear spontaneously and be brought to fruition through regular practice. In other cases, it may require strict attention and deliberate efforts to achieve a modicum of proficiency, but the attribute is inherent and it is there for discovery and development.

Throughout his experience as a science teacher, then as a university professor, and finally as a psychologist in private practice, Gregg never lost sight of the values he first expressed in his maverick candidate's statement. He marveled at how he had been inspired to write the statement at that time and with the risk involved. Yet, he somehow knew he was on the right track. In retrospect, he realized it was no coincidence and he was truly grateful for the guidance he had received from the Universal Mind.

CHAPTER V

Darkness Into Light

There can be no transforming of darkness into light and of apathy into movement without emotion.

--- Carl Gustav Jung

Entering the proverbial dark night

Despite steadily mounting acceptance by students, parents, and administrators of his new school, Gregg's marriage slowly began to unravel. The bad times started when the move was made from placid Sand Creek to the very different demands and opportunities of life on the edge of Chicago. His wife became increasingly withdrawn and morose. He stayed busy at his teaching job. He tried to make up the difference to their four daughters. His popularity in the community opened many opportunities for them. When it came to helping them participate, their mother was conspicuously absent. Their invitations to parties and other social events often went unanswered or got lost. No birthday parties, sleepovers, or study sessions were held at their house. He talked with other parents. He drove the girls to and from their appointments. She was always a little too tired, or sick, or couldn't see well enough to drive after dark. With little or no cooperation from their mother, the invitations gradually dried up.

Under these circumstances, Gregg experienced mounting stress. In the fall of 1957, the load became too great and his spleen went out of control. Instead of breaking down and recycling only worn out red blood cells, it ceased to discriminate and destroyed every red blood cell that came flowing through its domain. His treatment, although it gave him his third near death experience, was ultimately successful. As the anesthetic wore off after surgery to remove his spleen, he became profoundly depressed. Everything he had been juggling came crashing down. The pain of realizing that he had lost his wife (if he had ever really found her) and that their beautiful daughters were being seriously harmed was more than he could bear. In addition, he was out of money and medical benefits. He feared he couldn't make the mortgage payments and would lose the house. He felt very much alone and saw his life as a cruel joke. He grew ever more fearful about anything and everything. What little sleep he managed to get was increasingly fitful and only compounded his distress. He desperately tried to hang on to what his nurses had helped him understand, that love mattered and made a difference.

Desperately seeking help

Something within him said to trust and seek help. He called his internist and requested an immediate appointment. Sitting on the examination table in the doctor's office, he tried to describe what was happening with him. His emotions rose up with a vengeance and he was only able to cry uncontrollably for the next twenty minutes. He got a referral to another doctor who was both a neurologist and a psychiatrist. Their first meeting was in a conference room at the hospital where his spleen had been removed. He had to tough it out (waiting) for several painful hours until the doctor finished his rounds.

"Hi, I'm Dr. Moses."

"Gregg Emerson. Thanks for agreeing to see me. I need help bad. I can't hold on much longer."

"What seems to be the problem?'

"I've just had surgery; my spleen removed. I've got stitches from here to here. Being opened like that ....."

"Makes you feel invaded?"

"Yes. And I'm in a lot of pain and I'm afraid that I'll cough or get bumped and pull my stitches apart (sobs)."

"You feel like you are in constant danger?"

"Yes, And I can't sleep and I can't eat and I shake all the time."

"You feel like you're really coming unglued?"

"Yes. I don't think I can hold it together much longer (heaving sobs)."

"I really need some help with this quick or I'm going down the tubes."

"You want me to do something for you right away?"

"Yes. I can't work and I'm out of money and I can't feed my family or pay our mortgage. We'll lose our house soon and then what'll we do?"

"OK, I can put you in the hospital right now, where you'll be safe from injury and get help with your depression."

"Oh, no! I can't go in the hospital. I don't have any more medical benefits. We're out of money. There's nothing coming in for food and the other things they need."

"Then, you'll have to go back to your teaching job. Hospital or back to work. One or the other. What'll it be?"

"How can I possibly go back go my teaching job in this condition?"

"I think there's a way I can help you with that. If you are willing to try. First, I'll give you some medication to calm you down and relieve some of your depression; enough so you can think about your work. Second, I'll talk to your employers and make some special arrangements that will minimize the physical effort you'll need to make for awhile. Third, I will meet with you here for an hour every Sunday morning, after I finish my rounds, to work on your depression. Have we got a deal?"

"Well, it's not what I expected. I can see I was naïve to think that I would come here and meet with you and go home an hour later all fixed up. Yes. It's a deal. And I really do appreciate what you are doing. I'll make it work. I have to."

The special arrangements included one round trip each day to his second floor classroom. He had to bring a bag lunch and eat there during the lunch hour when the room was empty. His students were glad to have him back on the job. They helped him in every possible way. They lifted things. They got what was needed for the day's lab work out of the storage cabinets and set it up at his direction. They supervised clean up and put things away. Even kids who were normally "rowdy" gave him their support. It amazed him that his pain, physical and mental, was greatly reduced when he was working with his students. He had a plan and it was working. He eventually came to realize that setting up a plan and starting to work on it was one of the surest ways out of depression.

Bargaining for a new start

His first session with Dr. Moses, at the hospital on a quiet Sunday morning, was the beginning of a new life. He soon realized that despite his high intelligence and some noteworthy accomplishments, there was a lot in his background that made him very vulnerable in a crisis. He worried that this weakness might be permanent. He expected that his sessions with Dr. Moses would be terminated as soon as his depression lifted enough so he could get by on his own. What happened next was surely a profound example of serendipity. At their last session, Gregg described his fears and made a proposal that he somehow knew would be accepted.

"Good morning, Gregg."

"Good morning, Dr. Moses."

"How are you today?"

"In some ways, I'm feeling better. Whatever you did to convince the administrators at my school to go along with the plan, it worked. And the students couldn't be more helpful. Things are working out very well in that respect. I'm feeling better physically and my depression is slowly melting away. However, now I'm really afraid about something else."

"Mm. And what might that be?"

"It's clear to me now that there's a lot of unresolved stuff in my unconscious mind that made me take such a hard fall. It probably was why I got sick in the first place and why I got so depressed when I came out of the surgery. I'm afraid that I'm stuck with this stuff and I'll always be screwed up because of it. I'm hoping you'll tell me it doesn't have to be that way; that you can help me learn how to overcome it."

"Well, it isn't true that the bad experiences you've had must always run your life. You can learn about these things and you can learn how to manage them."

"Then, I'm hoping you'll stay with me and help me with this. I don't have any money to pay you right now, but if you can help me survive and develop the intelligence I know I have, I will be able to pay you someday. We can keep a record of what I owe and I will pay interest on it as if it was a loan."

"Mmmh. Tell you what. I think we can work out something here. I'm not too handy at fixing things around the house. My wife is always after me to fix something and when I can find the time she isn't too happy with my workmanship. You know about these things. You are a science teacher. You have been remodeling your own house. You said your grandfather was a contractor and you've always been around that kind of activity. If you can do some of the repair and maintenance stuff she wants me to do, I'll continue with our Sunday sessions. It'll be a kind of trade-off. You do that for me and I'll do this for you. OK?"

"When do I start?"

"I'll check with my wife and let you know at our next Sunday session."

Thus began a relationship that saw him through four years of therapy sessions with Dr. Moses. The sessions took place at the hospital almost every Sunday to start with. After a couple of years they gradually became less frequent. Gregg was in the Moses' home initially to fix things. Their interactions progressed to wide ranging discussions while work was being done. After a time there were invitations for meals and other family functions. Ultimately, he was given keys to the house and treated like they might have treated the son they didn't have.

In the fall of 1962, Gregg received a National Science Foundation grant for a special program at Michigan State University that led to a Masters Degree in Science Education. His school board also gave him a sabbatical leave with a stipend that made up most of the difference between the grant and his teaching salary. He moved his family into married housing on the campus and enrolled the girls in a school attached to the College of Education. The year was demanding for him and it was a huge success. There were very few social pressures for his wife. The girls had many interesting things to do in the housing complex and elsewhere on the campus. In the spring, his wife and family moved back to their suburban Chicago home. He stayed on at the university through the summer to complete his master's degree. One of his favorite professors called him in for a talk one day and strongly encouraged him to come back for a doctoral degree. The encouragement included offers of financial aid and part-time employment in the college.

Back home, his teaching job went smoothly during the 1963-64 school year. When he shared his professor's encouraging remarks with Dr. and Mrs. Moses they quickly supported the idea. They said he definitely should do it and even offered to lend him some money, if necessary, to make it feasible.

Enduring and recovering from some very painful losses

In the fall of 1964, Gregg rented their house again and moved his family back to Michigan State University. This time he and his wife were frequently invited to events with other doctoral candidates and their spouses. Things didn't always go well. His wife imagined that people were looking down on her because she didn't have a college degree. She often got into verbal confrontations with "those high and mighty bitches that think they're better than everybody else because they've got college degrees. Soon as you meet one, they start prying into where you went to college."

Another doctoral candidate who had become a close friend suggested that Gregg look into a program at a nearby Community College for his wife. He said she could start course work that could later become part of a college degree. He proposed that with something meaningful of her own to work on, there would be less tension in their house. Gregg got the program information and found a course of study in it that would provide training to work as a dental assistant; something she had often talked about wanting to do some day. She was excited and said she wanted to enroll in the program. The course work went smoothly and her instructors were very supportive. She was thrilled with her good test scores and written feedback on the papers she wrote. Gregg learned from his own dentist that there was a shortage of qualified assistants in the community. He realized that this situation might provide some realistic experience for his wife that would keep her productively engaged. He told his dentist that he knew where there was a person in training who might be willing to serve as his intern to get the hands-on experience. After he shared this information with his wife and she met with the dentist, a deal was struck. She seemed to be quite happy with this new interest and her accomplishments. In view of her good marks and her special internship, her faculty advisor offered to substitute a home study course in dental office management for her final exam. It included all the bookkeeping events and problems that might be encountered in a normal business year. She accepted the assignment and went to work on it with real excitement. Certification was a sure thing that would soon be accomplished. Her work went well for a time. Some of the bookkeeping problems were the real and frustrating kind where hours had to be spent trying to find the missing forty cents. All of those detours were successfully navigated until preparation of the year-end report. The more she worked, the more frustrated she became. She knew her advisor was leaving town the day after final exams. The time was running out for completing her work and getting it turned in. The pressure soon became too much for her. She stopped working, had some angry confrontations with the girls, and went to bed. When Gregg came in that evening and tried to rouse her so he could find out what was happening, she went into an abusive tirade.

"Unnnnh. Leave me alone."

"Are you OK?"

"No. I'm not OK and it's your goddamned fault. You got me into this. I never wanted it in the first place."

"What happened?"

"That goddamned program that sounded so good. It isn't worth shit. I've worked on it 'til I'm blue in the face and I can't make it come out. There's something wrong with it so it just won't work, no matter what I do."

"Why don't we look at it together? You've been working very hard and you've done so well, it would be a shame to lose it now. When I've been working on something for a long time, I get to the place where I miss stuff I can see easily at other times when I'm fresh and rested."

"You can take that whole program and go to hell for all I care. It's just another one of your goddamned schemes. You're the one who wanted this anyway. Well, it's all yours now. I'm through. You want it done, you do it. I'm not."

Faced with the loss of her certification and the implication of that for his already strained family life, Gregg sat down at his desk with her program to see what he could do to save it. Eighteen continuous hours later, he struck the correct final balance. He packed everything neatly in a big manila envelope. They had less than an hour to drive it over to the community college and hand it to her advisor. He called to tell the woman that the work was on its way. He then went to tell his wife what he had done and that her advisor was expecting her there with the completed work in twenty minutes. To his surprise, she quickly got ready and went with him. He waited in the car while she took the papers to her advisor's office. She came back beaming. She said her advisor looked over the work and found all of the key points in order. She received a warm hug and congratulations!

A major crisis passed. Basic issues covered over one more time. A little peace and quiet followed. However, the girls were beginning to exhibit negative effects of the stress they witnessed in their household. One day while Gregg was away, the oldest daughter brought home her boyfriend to discuss their future plans. After a loud and hostile confrontation with her mother, during which a favorite record album was broken over her head, she angrily left with the boyfriend and went to live with his family. She stayed there until they got married at the end of her senior year in high school. She was not present when Gregg received his Ph.D. He was deeply saddened by the loss.

In the fall of 1966, he started a new job as a professor of educational psychology at a university in downtown Chicago. His wife went to work as a dental assistant in a neighboring community. There was an uneasy truce between them. When they attempted to socialize with colleagues and their wives or friends, more often than not she imagined a slight by one of the other women and told them where to go. She became increasingly withdrawn and isolated. When she came home from work she stayed by herself and slept a lot. After a very loud and destructive fight with their second daughter, that girl left the house and moved in with a friend's family. The eldest of the two remaining daughters assumed much of the caregiver's role for her younger sister. Gregg and the girls shared the household chores and prepared the meals. He drove them wherever they needed to go. Then he learned from a counselor at the local high school that the girls were being physically abused when he wasn't home. He realized that serious harm was being done under the circumstances. He confronted his wife with this information and suggested that she seek professional help. She didn't deny the abuse. She said they were getting out of control and something had to be done.

"You and your goddamned schemes are the cause of all the trouble. I get so frustrated I could die. You make me do whatever I do to them. And I'm not going to any goddamned psychologist. It's your problem, *you* go and leave me out of it. I've had enough of this shit. I'm going to file for a divorce and you can have all of these crazy kids."

She had often threatened divorce when she felt challenged or wanted to be left alone. This time he said, "I think you're right; it's the best thing to do." They agreed to part peacefully. He was to move elsewhere. She would keep the house and the car. He would pay child support for the two girls who were still at home until he could secure adequate housing where they would not have to change schools. They got together with the girls and told them what they were about to do. The older of the two said, "That is the smartest decision you two have made in a long time." When Gregg said he would be moving into an apartment six or eight blocks up the street, the younger girl tearfully asked, "Will it be OK if I ride my bike up to see you sometimes?" At this point he wept uncontrollably for several minutes before he could answer, "absolutely."

For a short time it seemed that they were all pulling together and doing what was best under the circumstances. He knew she would later claim he had taken advantage of her with "another one of his goddamned schemes." To counteract that possibility he made arrangements for a lawyer well known as "one of the best in Chicago" to represent her.

Her depression soon got worse. She was fired from her first job and advised by her employer to get professional help. She got another job and after a few weeks announced that she was going to marry her boss soon after the divorce was final. She said she wanted Gregg to take the girls. He agreed and was in the process of renting a place big enough to accommodate the four of them when she tearfully reported that her new romance was over. She was also fired again. Divorce negotiations then took a very negative turn. She wanted the house sold and the proceeds turned over to her. She wanted the car paid for and the title placed in her name. She wanted clearance to move back to southern Indiana with the youngest girl. She wanted him to pay child support to her for this girl. She said she didn't care where the other two girls went as long as it was not in a house with him. She made it clear that she didn't want the responsibility. At the same time, she wanted him to be deprived of any kind of close relationship with his daughters.

The laws in Illinois at that time only allowed a wife to sue for divorce. Whatever were the agreements between the spouses, the husband had to allow her to file and claim she had been subjected to abuse by him. Under the prevailing law she had great leverage to negotiate for a punitive settlement. Even when all concerned knew it was not warranted by the facts. To end the nightmare, Gregg yielded to her demands and a divorce was granted. He was left with a large debt and his job. She did allow two of the girls to move in with his mother in Sand Creek while they finished high school. The youngest went with her mother. He paid child support for the three girls until each had graduated.

He found a small apartment. He borrowed household items from friends and went to live by himself. He was very lonely and thought his life was essentially over. He immersed himself in his work. He lost a lot of weight. He was depressed and very angry. He had to run five miles in the morning and five more at night just to keep his adrenaline at a level he could tolerate. His students worried about him and offered wonderful support. His only experience with marijuana was when a well-meaning young female student baked some "special" brownies to serve at a party she was hosting for him. She later confessed and said they were meant to help him relax and have a little fun for a change. With the support of his friends, including most importantly Dr. and Mrs. Moses, he slowly began to get his balance back.

Picking up and moving forward

Then Jenna entered his world. He first met her when she was a student in one of the classes he was teaching. She was an accomplished student. Very bright. Very organized. The best note taker he had ever seen. She got his every word into her notebook and soon had it all committed to memory. She aced every quiz or test he gave. And she protested against his teaching methods! They didn't match with what she had come to expect and was exceptionally good at. She was very surprised when he invited her and another student who thrived on his "experiential" methods to join him one day for lunch. He said that after enjoying some good food, at his expense, he had an important favor to ask of them. He said he wanted the two of them to share their divergent views in a discussion of their experience in his class. She, of course, was expected to be the loyal opposition. With his teaching schedule and their heavy course loads plus part-time work commitments, it was a long way into the next quarter before they actually got together. Right away after they sat down together she offered an apology, "I don't think I can be the loyal opposition for you anymore. I've had time to think about the effects of what you did with our class. I realized that I have been using what I learned there to deal with many of the challenges presented by a large organization like this university." After a long and productive discussion, the three of them parted as friends. She graduated and left the campus to teach Sociology in a large suburban high school. The other student also graduated and went to teach creative English in a different high school. Gregg felt very much enriched by the earnest sharing of their ideas for improving his teaching.

A year later, Jenna came back to the campus during the summer after her first year of teaching to work as a research assistant for one of his colleagues. Gregg saw her in a hallway and asked her about her year as a new teacher. That discussion led to an invitation for coffee and some more friendly talk. They obviously enjoyed each other's company. The colleague, who was a close friend to Gregg and fully aware of his marital situation, noticed their compatibility. She suggested that he consider Jenna as a marriage partner. His response was quick and negative. "I like her a lot. She is very sensible and wonderful company. But she is much too young for me." His colleague quickly replied, "Don't be silly, she is a very mature young woman and your equal in any way you can name." With that sanction from a trusted friend, he made his move. After a few months of dating, he proposed and she accepted.

Jenna. Nineteen years younger than himself. Jewish. City born and raised. One of a kind. She had never been out of a city environment before he took her to meet his extended family in Sand Creek. Even when she had traveled by air to New York and the Bahamas, she got on and off the plane in city situations. A few miles south of Chicago, on that first trip to his mother's house through the flat and open Indiana farmland, he noticed that she seemed uneasy. When he asked what was on her mind she said, "There's nobody out here." However, she quickly adapted to the givens of his extended family in the rural context of southern Indiana. His relatives warmly accepted her very friendly demeanor and included her in family activities. They also let him know they thought he was, "a very lucky man."

Being quite adaptable and able to acknowledge the learning of something new and different, Jenna became proficient at engaging her own students in experiential learning. She guided them into situations where they learned to evaluate existing information as well as how to create valid new information. She had them engaged in such first-hand activities in real-life locations all around the Chicago area. A favorite was analyzing survey data they collected from passengers at O'Hare International Airport.

Several years later, she wrote an article that was published in a special feature of the Chicago Tribune that reflected on the negative to positive change in her relationship with her former teacher:

> I was studying to be a teacher and I really had very
> negative feelings about the teaching methods used by a

professor of my very first education course. I was a college sophomore and I vocalized my views so frequently during class and during visits to his office that I earned the label of "the loyal opposition." Much to my surprise, as I continued through the teacher education program, completed student teaching, and began my high school teaching career much of what he had taught me became the basis of my own lesson designs. The summer after my first year of teaching, I worked for another professor at my alma mater and I had the opportunity to have many extended conversations with my former professor. I shared my new found enthusiasm for group work, active learning, self-evaluation and the like. I discovered that his methods had put me in touch with my own strengths as a learner, and I, in turn, was able to give the same gift to my students. They became producers and evaluators of information, not merely absorbers of facts. The original negative vibrations became so positive that we were married that October and are still each other's biggest fans some 23 years later. I owe much of my success, as a teacher and now as an assistant principal to those strategies he offered me when I thought I already knew it all.

In time, Gregg came to realize that his dark night was not an ending. It was the stage before a marvelous new beginning. There were many synchronistic events. People appeared in his life to offer him love and support at just the right moments. And each time they did the darkness lifted a little. He became aware of the healing light up ahead and knew that he could get to it if he tried.

A growth producing turn-about

Twenty years after their fortuitous meeting in the hospital where Gregg had his spleen removed, Dr. Moses contracted a terminal illness. He was confined to that same hospital during a long drawn out period of diagnosis. Gregg was a regular visitor to his room where they discussed many important issues. When the diagnosis was complete and the prognosis was definitely terminal, Dr. Moses requested to be moved to his home. For some time he was able to move about the house, work on putting his affairs in order, and take his meals in the dining room. Gregg continued to be a frequent visitor. He fixed things around the house for Mrs. Moses. He went out for special purchases. He engaged in discussions with Dr. Moses who was always profoundly wise and thoughtful even under these trying conditions. Gradually, his disease progressed and his strength diminished. A hospital bed was brought into a quiet bedroom at the end of a narrow hallway. He reluctantly moved there to conserve his strength. A full-time nurse was employed to assist Mrs. Moses in meeting his needs. His meals were served at his bedside. He deeply appreciated the care that was being taken to look after him and keep him comfortable. Even so, he let it be known that he dearly missed being able to eat with his wife and friends out in the sunny dining room. Knowing that he felt isolated and confined touched Gregg deeply. It energized his creative thinking. He came up with a plan that would allow Dr. Moses' bed to be rolled into the dining room and up to the table whenever he felt like it.

The plan was both simple and complex. Their living room was on the other side of the east wall of the bedroom where he was confined. And the large open dining room extended from the east side of the living room. If the wall between the bedroom and the living room were removed, his bed could easily be rolled through half of the house. Simple to remove the wall. He had determined that it was not a load bearing structure. Just put a plaster cutting blade in his electric hand saw and cut away. Complex to get the go-ahead from Mrs. Moses who was very protective of her husband and very fussy about her house. She trusted Gregg because her experience with him was that he always found a good way to fix whatever she requested. And he was neat about it. This time she was most worried about how the dust from cutting the plaster would affect Dr. Moses who would be in his bed a few feet from the wall. Gregg assured her that he would surround the entire operation with heavy plastic sheeting and keep the dust contained within that enclosure. She asked Dr. Moses what he thought of the idea. He heartily approved. She reluctantly gave the OK for Gregg to proceed and went to the kitchen where she wouldn't have to watch. At that point Gregg realized there might be some unanticipated electrical or plumbing pipes in the wall that might keep the plan from working. He started to sweat. He put on a painter's mask and went inside the plastic bubble to start sawing the plaster. The heat and lack of ventilations made him sweat even more. He carefully followed the lines he had drawn to guide his cutting. He wanted a snug fit to the wide trim boards he would install over the rough edges of the opening. When painted to match the other trim the new opening would look as if it belonged there. Periodically, he checked with Dr. Moses to see how he was handling the noise. He said he was fine and appeared to be entertained by the whole process.

When all of the plaster was removed, Gregg breathed a great sigh of relief. No electric wires or other mechanical obstructions were located in the wall. He carefully cut away the wood studs and then installed the previously painted trim boards around the opening. The plastic bubble was removed. Voila! Dr. Moses was a free man. Mrs. Moses was a "wreck." She had behaved like a trooper throughout the changeover. Even when a *little* dust escaped from the bubble and made it necessary to move some of the living room furniture. However, nobody was happier to see the work finished than Gregg himself.

Eventually, Dr. Moses' illness progressed beyond the ability of his wife and the nurse to meet his growing needs. He felt it would be best to return to the hospital where medical personnel would be available around the clock. Gregg continued to visit him on a regular basis. Their discussions became labored, with long periods of silence. Nevertheless, they remained thoughtful and pertinent. One day a nurse who had been attending Dr. Moses for some time stopped Gregg in the hall after his visit and asked to speak with him. Her words were filled with compassion and concern. She said she had observed the behavior of his many visitors and Gregg was the only one who still treated him with recognition that he was aware of everything and could still respond thoughtfully if given time. She felt that most of those who visited him, including his deeply concerned family, mistook his slowness to respond as evidence that he really wasn't there. They talked over him and around him as if he were already gone. "I just wanted to let you know how much he appreciates your company." Dr. Moses' slowing responses were gradually replaced by a state of peaceful repose. From there he quietly stopped breathing and slipped away.

Mrs. Moses asked Gregg to speak at his funeral. He felt honored and apprehensive. He started to sweat just thinking about what he might say. There would be lots of Dr. Moses' powerful friends and colleagues in attendance. This was an even bigger challenge than cutting out the wall in his house. He tried several times to write a eulogy like those he had read or witnessed at other funerals. His frustration mounted. Finally, he dropped all conventional approaches and wrote just what he was feeling. He delivered it as he felt it, slowly, deeply passionate, and with powerful pauses that spoke volumes in the silent spaces:

Perhaps you can imagine....

> A man with great respect for learning
> A man who is an avid learner himself
> Who constantly pursues knowledge of the world – its history, its art, its music, its traditions, its peoples; of humankind and the human condition
> A man who reads profusely and thinks profusely
> Who seeks truth and understanding
> A stimulating man who elevates the level of discussion

Perhaps you can imagine….

A man with inner wisdom
A sagacious man who develops significant perspectives
from his life experience
A mature man who is able to care about others
Who is able to be a good friend
A man who is secure enough within himself to be able to
appreciate the goodness in others

Perhaps you can imagine….

A man of compassion
Who is able to be truly concerned with the needs of other
human beings
Who is a healing man
Who is a caring man
A man who is willing and able to use his personal gifts in
the service of others

Perhaps you can imagine….

A truly generous man
Who often extended a helping hand to individuals in their
hour of need
Who consistently gives a measure of his time and energy
and financial resources to support humane causes
Who frequently provides economic support for promising
students
Who makes the substantial and continuing contributions
necessary to help found a major university

Perhaps you can imagine….

A man who inspires people to develop the best in
themselves
Who encourages
Who supports
Who helps people to see new possibilities
Who by his realness and his own enlightenment generates
in others the desire to be and do better

Perhaps you can recognize....

That my good friend Dr. Jeffrey Moses was such a man

His voice cracked a little at one point while he was speaking. He consoled himself by thinking that it was real and probably appropriate under the circumstances. He was profoundly saddened by the loss of his friend and mentor. The personal support and learning opportunities were irreplaceable. However, he realized that something very positive was happening within himself. A metamorphosis was under way. In the process of aiding Dr. Moses their roles were irrevocably switched. He ceased to seek comfort as the subordinate receiver and willingly volunteered himself in compassionate service.

Finding great rewards in program development and teaching

Gregg had long dreamed of being part of a university. He believed that universities were places where searching for the truth was first and foremost. He was aware that tenure provisions had been created to insure that truth seekers were protected from the whims and politics of the marketplace. One could earn a decent living while seeking to make creative contributions to the world. Safe and unmolested. Stimulated by an environment of fellow truth seekers where new ideas were generated and shared for the good of mankind. A refuge for serious learners and dedicated producers of new and improved information.

When he moved to the university level, Gregg devised many experiences to help prospective teachers *see outside of the box*. He had a lot of fun with one such experience that he devised to stir up their creative imaginations. Right away, after introductions and housekeeping chores were completed, he took his new students up to the top of the tallest building on the campus where they could look out of the windows for a panoramic view of the city. He asked them to study the scene before them and record what they saw. He then took them to a conference room, organized them into small groups, and asked them to share with each other what they had observed. Each group was then asked to list on large sheets of newsprint the different features identified and the number of times it was mentioned in their observation notes. These lists were posted around the room. He then asked each group to select one person to present their list. Their reports were comprehensive. The observers saw many features of the scene before them: cars, trucks, trains, buses, streets, buildings, underpasses, overpasses, sizes, shapes, colors, shading, building materials, people, and activities. There was even some interesting speculation about what the buildings contained. However, they almost always missed noticing the round wooden water tanks on top of the numerous shorter buildings in the older sections of the city.

Gregg made a few comments about the interesting variety of their observations. Then he said he was going to show them something unique out there that all (or most of them) had missed. Something that would make it impossible for them to ever see the scene in the same way again. When the students were assembled back at the windows, he pointed out the water tanks. He noted that there were thousands of them. He said they were installed on top of every new building before people learned how to build skyscrapers. Water was pumped up to the tanks at night and was available by gravity during the day. Later, when buildings were constructed higher than 10 floors, they couldn't use a water tank on top of the building. The water pressure from the pull of gravity would exceed the strength of the plumbing materials. He pointed out (*with dramatic emphasis*) that even if stronger pipes were devised and it was possible to turn on a faucet at the bottom of a pipe 30 stories tall, the stream would probably drill a hole right through the sink. Newer buildings have an internal tank every 10 floors. Water is still pumped up at night, only 10 floors at a time. Improvements in the city water pressure and booster pumps eventually made the old rooftop storage tanks obsolete. Many were emptied and unhooked. They are now clean and dry inside. Then he said, "just so you will never be able to look out on the scene again without seeing those tanks, here is something to stimulate your imaginations. Suppose the hippies in town discovered these tanks, found a way to get up to them, and moved in. Little penthouses on top of the city. Rent free!"

A variation to supplement and reinforce their changed perspective was to have them stand at the windows and imagine what the city would look like if everything was dissolved away except the plumbing systems which stayed right where they were at the time. Or everything but the electrical wires. These exercises at seeing things differently got his classes focused on ways to see beyond their existing views. With a little guidance he was able to move them into discussions about what to teach and how to teach it.

Out of the animated discussions that followed these experiences, plans were made to design a new teacher education program based on experiential learning. Their ideas were brought to the attention of other faculty members who also found them exciting and offered to help develop such a program. Faculty in public and parochial schools were contacted for their thinking about how teacher education could be improved. Many of them were pleased to be included. They offered to let prospective teachers observe and work with students in their classrooms throughout their involvement in the program. They wanted them to have lots of experiential learning before student teaching during their senior year. From the exchange of information between these interested groups, a Cooperative Program in Urban

Teacher Education was developed. With lots of observations and opportunities to work with children in real classroom situations, there was plenty to discuss in education classes back on campus. Eventually, the entire teacher education program was revised to incorporate the new design that started with students *thinking outside the box.*

Politics began to corrupt the academic environment

After ten years of very rewarding efforts within the bounds of that perspective, Gregg was deeply disappointed to learn that this dream was being aborted at the university where he worked. Politics were beginning to replace integrity and the quest for truth. Tenure still protected faculty positions but other ways were being employed to put a damper on those who were viewed as too independent. Teaching assignments and class loads could make the difference between a satisfying work life and a frustrating overload. Salary increases were being used to reward "team players" and serve others notice of their diminished valuation. Reduction of essential secretarial support made it difficult to keep up with academic demands. Office space was reassigned on the basis of the Dean's selection of winners and losers. For instance, one of Gregg's colleagues was reassigned to share an office with a man who was a constant smoker. The "shared" office smelled like the smoking car on a commuter train. The move was made to serve notice: "get with the program or go away." These changes were more than Gregg wanted to accept. He loved the university setting and truly enjoyed working with his students as they engaged with the metropolitan community. As he increasingly witnessed them being treated as ciphers in a scheme where the primary goal was political power for a few misguided professors, he decided that he needed to remove himself from the scene. He was very sad to see the dream fade away to a new reality that was negative and destructive. It was somewhat satisfying to learn that after he left two successive Deans were censured for their unethical conduct and removed from their administrative positions.

Despite his genuine love for teaching, great relationships with students, and tenured status as an associate professor, Gregg's wife recognized that campus politics were making it increasingly difficult for him to continue there without compromising his integrity. In view of his distress, she suggested that he leave. What's more, she committed to being the primary breadwinner; forever, if necessary. This was not idle talk. She had an excellent position, and, although 19 years younger, had already begun to earn more than he did. They realized that through Post Graduate courses and supervised practice to upgrade his teaching and organizational skills he had accumulated the equivalent of a second doctoral degree in psychology. Over the next three years they both put a great deal of effort into getting him ready to attain certification as a clinical psychologist. She even brushed up on statistics so that she could re-teach him the basics he needed to pass the state exam.

Moving to bypass irrational and unethical developments

He passed the exam, left the university and began a part-time private practice that was everything they had hoped for. It was stimulating, rewarding, growth producing, and free from layers of hierarchy. Income was marginal but that never once became an issue. There were other special benefits. Jenna had the opportunity to fully develop her career. He developed an extraordinary relationship with their growing daughter as a result of being her primary caregiver. There was increased discretionary time for the entire family. Most of all, there was an exponential increase in trust and closeness Jenna and Gregg developed toward each other. That is not to say that things always went smoothly. There were bumps in the road. Problems came up and were treated as challenges to be met constructively. There was always a commitment to work toward understanding and finding ways to develop good resolutions for all concerned. This perspective was passed to their daughter by watching her parents apply it and by her own experiential learning.

Deciding to write and share

Under these circumstances he also had time to think about his unique life experiences. He decided to collect his thoughts and insights in writing. He felt there were things he could share with others that could make an important difference in their lives. His home office was up high on the second floor. It overlooked a broad green swale that a heavy rain sometimes made into a temporary lake. When it was dry, wild deer often wandered into the scene and looked for something to eat. With that verdant and tranquil view through the window over his desk it was a special place to read and think and write. He read and thought and wrote a lot over the next fifteen years. Eventually, he started to wind down his psychotherapy practice and moved his office to a suitable room in their house. His daughter was a busy student in nearby schools and his involvement with her was more to counsel than administer. She did very well at sports and he was thrilled by her performances in the gym and on the field. She played center on the junior high girls basketball team that had the first league championship in the school's history. In high school she was a versatile volleyball player and won recognition as an all-conference hurdler. Her academic accomplishments were equally proficient. She also served on various school governance committees. At home he taught her to use hand tools, including his drills and electric saws. When he decided to enclose the underside of their backyard deck, he called out measurements and she cut all of the cedar trim boards to order. She had often accompanied him to the local hardware and home improvement stores. She learned about their wares while riding in shopping carts when she was small and by going alone for something he needed after she learned to drive. Witnessing her growth and development, while being her primary caregiver during those formative years, was a source of great joy. That joy was compounded as he observed his wife providing developmental balance by tending to their daughter's knowledge of the social graces, fashion protocols, and life management skills. In retrospect, he realized that his partnership with Jenna was another instance of serendipity in his life and a very precious gift that was not offered to most men in his culture.

CHAPTER VI

Receiving Guidance

The Spirit comes gently and makes himself known by his fragrance. He is not felt as a burden, for he is light, very light. Rays of light and knowledge stream before him as he approaches. The Spirit comes with the tenderness of a true friend and protector to save, to heal, to teach, to counsel, to strengthen, to console. The Spirit comes to enlighten the mind first of one who receives him, and then, through him, the minds of others as well. As light strikes the eyes of a man who comes out of the darkness into sunshine and enables him to see clearly things he could not see before, so light floods the soul of a man counted as worthy of receiving the Holy Spirit and enables him to see things beyond the range of human vision, things hitherto undreamed of.

---1 Corinthians 12:6-7, 27

As the plane hummed on toward Seattle, Gregg felt as if he were strapped into a time capsule. The metal cocoon of the plane's cabin, filled to capacity with all kinds of people, confined his body to a very limited space. Yet, he was able to travel throughout time and space in his mind. He never ceased to marvel at these wonderful planes. Gigantic creations made of wires and metal and fabric that harnessed the energy of the sun to defy gravity. Enter one of the magnificent capsules someplace. Shut the door and strap yourself in. Rest, read, eat, sleep, meditate, and explore your inner mind. Later, when the crew says it's time, and opens the door, you come alert and step outside into someplace else.

Rapidly changing perspectives

While exploring within his inner mind he found it easy to shift back and forth from one place to another. Recent events and experiences seemed to merge with what had happened in other time frames. In fact, time didn't seem to matter much. What did seem important was how it all fit together. How he had evolved since arriving on the earth. The guidance he received from both human and spiritual sources. The person he was becoming. Learning about universal love. The profound significance of events that seemed quite mundane at the time they happened. The joy that approached rapture when their true meaning was discovered and changed his perspective. Realizing that they were no coincidence.

No coincidence. Those two words kept repeating over and over in his mind. No coincidence. No coincidence. Something very timely that happened because it was needed to bring a message, bring a life challenge into focus, or reveal a new perspective. Something manifested or influenced by unseen forces in the universe. Forces or entities that he felt all people could learn to be aware of, if they paid careful attention. He was convinced of this because the more he paid attention, the more he could recall potent examples from his past. He was also more aware when they happened in the present. He began to count on them and deeply appreciated the opportunities they presented. They were never coercive or frightening. Just helpful access to interesting and useful information. What he did with the information was always left to his discretion.

The Muzak stopped playing and was replaced by the captain's voice. He said that the plane was on an incoming glide path to the Seattle airport and would be landing soon. The seat belt sign was turned on. He asked that food trays be folded up and secured. Also that passenger seatbacks be returned to their upright positions. The flight attendants came up the aisles, systematically retrieving leftover containers and reminding the passengers to do as the captain requested. As the nose of the plane started to tilt more sharply downward, the attendants took their seats up front and strapped themselves in. Shortly, a piercing screech signaled that the plane's tires had contacted the runway at very high speed. Reversing the engines provided an enormous thrust against the forward momentum of the plane. Its speed was soon reduced to something more compatible with the status of a heavily loaded vehicle in crowded space on the ground. He always loved that part of the flight. He marveled at the fantastic human accomplishments that allowed precision management of so much power. He could *feel* it as well as see it. He was really enthralled by the miracle of these planes.

He was glad that his assignment in Seattle would be concluded that week. He had enjoyed working in the great northwest. A very different culture. In many ways it was more laid back than his home base in Chicago. Magnificent natural surroundings. Coffee shops everywhere. Good coffee for the most part. The place swam in coffee. Maybe it was a good way to cope with the frequent rainy weather and overcast days. He would soon be going back to the hustle of Chicago. That ramblin' town. Where the action is. The navel of the Midwest. When he and his second wife had lived for a year in Washington, D.C., they found a new appreciation for Chicago as the center of things. The clerks in various department stores in and around the capital often said to them, "We don't carry that in stock but we can get it for you from Chicago." All of the good and special stuff was in Chicago and had to be imported. Including Uno's deep-dish pizza and Chicago style hot dogs. They considered refunding Gregg's sabbatical leave stipend and staying in Washington to open a Chicago style hot dog stand. They had discussed it seriously with some friends who were formerly from Chicago and whose employment with a U.S. Senator was soon to terminate. The difficulty in consistently obtaining fresh supplies from Chicago, such as Vienna Beef Products and Rosen's poppy seed buns, dealt a fatal blow to the otherwise promising fantasy.

When Gregg got back to Chicago, he continued to be visited with events of synchronicity (no coincidence). His awareness of such things was greatly expanded by a series of challenging experiences that included precognitive and out-of-body dreaming. The first occurred in December of 1996, shortly after the death of his mother. He was unusually sensitized after reading several books on the subject. He had listened for many hours as his mother haltingly described her own near-death experience after she tumbled down some stairs in a diabetic coma. She said she hadn't told anyone else because she was afraid they would think she was crazy. Although she had not heard of such things or read about them, the experiences she described meshed perfectly with those described in the books that had captured Gregg's attention. The long tunnel. The brilliant light that you could stare into without blinking. The feelings of complete safety and unconditional love. She experienced it all. And he felt privileged to have her share it with him.

During the week after her death, Gregg stayed in her house for three days while he made funeral arrangements and prepared to settle her estate. When he entered the house late the first night he had the strong sensation that someone was in the house with him. He made a visual inspection of the premises and found no people or animals. Yet the feeling that he wasn't alone persisted. He went upstairs to bed in the room he had so often occupied during his visits. Being very tired he was quickly asleep. About 3:00 a.m. he was suddenly awakened by someone kneeling on the bed. Then he felt someone bend over him and kiss him gently on the cheek. At the same time he received an unmistakable message from his mother that let him know she was O.K. At first he was afraid to open his eyes. When he finally summoned up the courage to do it and turned on the light, he saw no one. He fell back asleep and when he woke up two hours later he no longer had the sensation of someone or something in the house with hm. He stayed two more nights in the big empty house and never felt that way again.

That experience changed him. Afterward, there was something about him that certain other people somehow recognized. They easily took him into their confidence and told him about experiences similar to his that they had kept to themselves for many years. He knew and they knew that there was more in the world than could be seen. Their common experiences made them realize they could be aware of whatever it was, and communicate with it, and even get help from it.

Discovering the Universal Mind

Several months before his mother's death Gregg had registered for the 8th International Conference of the National Council on Clinical Application of Behavioral Medicine. It was scheduled for December 9 – 16, 1996, at Hilton Head Island in South Carolina. About two weeks before the conference he had a powerful and confusing dream. In this dream there were two spiritual entities that he was keenly aware of but couldn't see. They told him that he would find everything he needed to know in the "condign of his magnetic cubature." There was such power in this gift from the two entities that he got up and wrote the words on a scrap of paper. He then went back to sleep and forgot about the dream. The scrap of paper was inadvertently tossed in a wastebasket. The next afternoon the dream came back to him but he couldn't remember the message. He went to look for his notes and panicked because he remembered it was a regular cleaning day at his house. On cleaning day morning all of the wastebaskets were routinely emptied into a trashcan and placed outside for pick-up by a trash service. However, the cleaning person had called in sick that day (a rare occurrence) and after rummaging through the wastebaskets for an hour he found what he had written. It didn't make sense to him. He had never heard of those words. Neither had his wife Jenna who was a crossword puzzle expert with a voluminous vocabulary. He asked some friends with the same result. Something urged him to keep looking. In a large dictionary at the local public library he found obscure definitions for the words that let him know he was on to something special, although he was still confused about what it was.

Clarity came when he met Dr. Valerie Hunt at the conference and learned about her work with human vibrations and energy fields. He came to the conference scheduled to be in a Post Conference Master Class with the renowned clairvoyant and healer, Caroline Myss. She became ill and was not able to keep her commitment. He was asked to make another choice. Intuition guided him to select Dr. Hunt's substituted Master Class on the Science of Human Vibrations.

The night before the class Gregg had another very powerful dream. He was in a familiar house and the occupants asked his opinion on how to replace their living room floor. On close examination, he found that the supporting beams were badly decayed and needed to be replaced as well. Then the dream shifted to their backyard where an enormous and very powerful steam locomotive sat on a track that went across the yard and up a small hill. At the base of the hill there was a gap in the track. He could not see over the hill or where the track went on the other side. He released some steam into the massive engine and moved the locomotive forward. When it reached the gap in the tracks it was necessary to apply a lot more energy to move the locomotive across the gap and up the hill toward the unknown over the horizon. Intuition encouraged him to drive on despite the obvious risk.

In Dr. Hunt's class the next day she asked for volunteers to lay on a table so she could demonstrate how to check a person's energy field. Gregg was moved to be one of the first. When she held the diagnostic pendulum over him she exclaimed to the group, "Wow! This guy is really alive (has enormous energy). Nothing keeps him down." Then, almost in a whisper she added, "when it ever does he will be finished with this life." And bending over him so no one else could hear she said, "You have to find a way to do something with your energy soon."

His experience in Dr. Hunt's Master Class was unexpected and profound. When she guided the participants through meditation exercises his body jerked and jumped about as if energy currents were passing through him. Each time he meditated during the next several months he experienced these involuntary movements. As time passed they gradually became less intense. He became increasingly calm and peaceful. Several times he reached higher levels of awareness and had powerful insights into ancient experiences that illuminated his current issues. Clarity of his preconference dream also came as a result of learning about human vibrations and energy fields under her guidance. Cubature was defined as "the determination of the cubic contents of a thing." The definition of condign was, "well deserved: fitting; adequate." Freely translated, the condign of one's magnetic cubature described the unique contents (information) of their energy field. His dream had happened before he had any knowledge of human energy fields. He had never heard of Dr. Hunt or her work before the conference. He was certain that the events that placed him in her class were no coincidence. With that experience and the subsequent reading of her outstanding book, *Infinite Mind: The Science of Human Vibrations,* his awareness took a quantum leap.

Making extraordinary perceptual journeys

As his spiritual awareness and development moved along, Gregg sometimes found that during extraordinary dream states he was transported over great distances. His somnambulate trips defied gravity, normal physical requirements, and the usual limitations of time. At first he was convinced that the travels were truly the kind of out-of-body experiences he had read about, where his physical body actually moved from one location to another. The scenes were so vivid and his senses were activated as if what he was experiencing was real. Later, he learned that it was his expanded perception that made these fascinating journeys. His physical body remained sleeping and dreaming in place. He was fully aware of environmental details when he perceived distant places and things in such vivid dreams. Others could not see him or hear him speak. However, they were often acutely aware of his perceptual presence. Telepathic communication and the transfer of healing energy to receptive individuals were easily accomplished by simply managing his thoughts.

Although he was becoming quite comfortable with spiritual phenomena, the first of these transcendent travel experiences was initially a bust. In a very powerful dream he decided to pay a visit to a dear friend who lived more than twenty miles away. He arose from his sleeping body feeling very much awake and alert. He quietly dressed and went downstairs. At that point he noticed that he was in a standing position but his feet weren't touching the floor. He found he could move about at will just by thinking the moves he wanted to make. Out through the front door and up the street as if he were traveling in some sort of invisible vehicle. In this fashion he traveled through the streets that led to the tollway. On the tollway he continued to travel as if he were standing a few feet above the pavement. He could feel the wind in his face as he moved along. His speed and direction were easily controlled by his thoughts. However, when he arrived at her house he was not well received. It was clear that she was alone and extremely distressed by the knowledge that someone or something unseen was there with her. The closer he came the more she was afraid. Although she had become quite comfortable with their telepathic communications this mode of contact was completely new and he had not talked with her about anything like it. Instead of the friendly reunion he anticipated, his visit in this unusual manner was causing real fear in his friend. He quickly retreated from the premises and started back to his home. Up the driveway in his invisible traveling bubble. Quickly moving onto the tollway. And then a surprise! As he moved along the tollway way he was aware of company traveling with him. They were also traveling in a standing position. They were out at the front edge of the light that preceded him much like auto headlights on the roadway. He couldn't see them clearly but he *knew* they were there. They weren't threatening. In fact, it seemed that they were with him to see that he had a safe trip back to his house. Gliding around the tollway exit. Down the main street of his village and into his subdivision. Moving as a spirit might move. Into his driveway. Passing through the still-closed front door. Up the stairs to his bedroom. Then back into his sleeping body. When he woke up later in the usual way these events were clearly in his memory. He got up and wrote them down.

Next day he called his friend Kate to discuss his dream. When she answered she was obviously shaken. She said she had been alone in her house the past night when she became aware that someone or something was on the premises with her. It was so powerful she turned on all of the lights, including the yard lights. The feeling persisted. She got so scared that she got down beside her bed and started to pray. Se kept the lights on all night and got very little sleep. When Gregg told her about his dream she was not amused. She was somewhat relieved to know that he was the intruding presence. At the same time she said she had been very much afraid and didn't want to experience such feelings again, especially when she was home alone. She was fascinated by the fact that both of them could be tuned in to the same vivid dream. It verified that they could communicate with each other by telepathic means. That much she found exciting. He assured her that if there were any future contacts of that nature he would identify himself at the outset. She asked for time to think about it. She felt she needed to process her thoughts and feelings. She thought she could do that much better with some distance between them for a while. He agreed and said he would wait for her to get in touch with him. Several weeks went by before he got her call.

In the summer of 1977 Gregg went to Spain with his wife and daughter. They flew to Barcelona where they spent a few pleasant days. Then they took an overnight sleeper train to Madrid. In Madrid they rented a car and traveled in a giant loop throughout the southern half of the country. Eventually they returned to Madrid for a flight home. It was during the final nights of their stay in Madrid that Gregg had two more out-of-body dream experiences. In the first of these he found himself exiting his sleeping body and floating upward. He felt totally alert and curious. He continued to float upward through the roof of the hotel and high into the atmosphere above the city. He was quite comfortable even though he was at an altitude where he knew he would normally be freezing and unable to breathe. Looking down from the great height he hoped he didn't wake up and lose his ability to be safely where he was. Next he found himself turning toward the United States. Once he was oriented to a destination there, he began traveling toward it at a very high velocity that he knew was impossible within normal parameters of time and distance. When he reached the United States he realized he was going to the home of his special friend Kate. Over her house near Chicago he descended in the same gentle way that he had left the hotel in Spain. As he neared her house a large ball of brilliant white light joined him and went with him through the roof. It then expanded until it found her sleeping peacefully and suffused her with healing energy. She later said she calmly received it because she somehow knew it was a gift from Gregg and that he was O.K. Then he ascended as he had arrived. He found himself again high in the atmosphere and oriented toward the hotel in Spain. The trip back was like the trip over, comfortable and swift, to a point above the city of Madrid. Then a slow, safe descent back into his sleeping body in the hotel room. A fascinating night's work! Upon his return to the United States Gregg called his friend Kate to chat about his trip and ask if she had received any *special* messages while he was gone. She told him she was aware that he had visited her as before but she wasn't frightened at all this time. She said it was clear to her that he was there in spirit and just wanted to let her know that he was O.K.

A second dream occurred in the same manner while he was staying in Madrid. He again floated upward from his sleeping body into a region of the atmosphere normally inhospitable to unprotected human beings. He then traveled swiftly to another destination in the United States. This time he found himself over the home of a former client who had been diagnosed with multiple sclerosis. She had come to him some months earlier for therapy to help her manage her feelings of stress and depression related to this debilitating illness. As he neared her house the ball of brilliant white light joined him as before. He descended into the house where he found her asleep. Without any communication he released the healing energy of the light to surround her and flow into her body. Then he retreated upward from where she was located in the house, turned toward Spain, and began his journey back to Madrid. He arrived over the hotel and slowly drifted down through the roof and upper floors of the building. He then slid back into his sleeping body. This dream experience, like the other one originating in Madrid, happened in the wee hours of the morning. It seemed much more realistic than a regular dream. He could see and touch and feel as if he were wide awake. When he got back to his home office he called this client to tell her he was back in town and inquire about her progress. During their chat about her current condition she didn't mention his *visit* but she told him she was feeling much better and had just arrived back home after a surprisingly good workout at a local health club.

CHAPTER VII

A Cosmic Point of View

There are no unnatural or supernatural phenomena, only very large gaps in our knowledge of what is natural....

---Edgar Mitchell

After several years of searching for a system of orientation and devotion that he could respectfully use to guide his life, Gregg found what he was looking for in a Unitarian Fellowship at the State University in Rockton. He was a second semester sophomore at the time. He was also employed part-time as a bookkeeper by one of the owners of an industrial stone quarry near the University. His employer was Jewish by birth but, like Gregg, he was earnestly making a search for a more satisfying religious system to guide his life. In frequent discussions during break times and during their car trips from Sand Creek to the quarry office they both realized that their interests in this respect were very much alike. Eventually, this realization led to an invitation to accompany his boss to a Unitarian Fellowship meeting on the university campus. The open and thoughtful exchange of ideas at that meeting induced Gregg to make a comprehensive search of information about the Unitarian Church. What he found convinced him that this approach to religious thought was what he had been searching for. When he later moved to Chicago to take a new teaching job, he located a very active Unitarian Church group near his suburban home and enrolled his family.

In 1961 the Unitarians merged with the Universalists, a group that held similar views abut religious education and practice. The names of both groups were incorporated into the inclusive title: Unitarian/Universalist. Looking back on the events that got him into active membership and enabled him to learn so much significant information he had to realize, once again, that serendipity was a potent factor. As Gregg's numerous positive learning experiences within the Unitarian/Universalist community rolled by on the screen in his mind, he recalled the installation of a great painting in the sanctuary of the church he attended. It covered a portion of the south wall from floor to ceiling. It was 5 feet wide and 20 feet tall. The painting was titled "Darkness Into Light," with dark and turbulent colors at the bottom giving way to ever lighter and brighter colors as the eye moved upward. It signified enlightenment through learning. He remembered his fascination with this wonderful painting and how it influenced him to do a great deal of thinking about human evolution toward the light of awareness.

For several years Gregg had recorded his insights as soon as possible after they came to him. He quickly wrote them down on whatever he could find at the moment. Old envelopes, the backs of grocery lists, the margins of magazine pages, legal pads; even on the palm of his hand. If he had access to a tape recorder, he would put the information on tape while it was still fresh and vivid in his mind. Later he would listen and put what he had said into writing. All of these notes were put into file folders for safekeeping. Periodically he would review what was in the folders and write about each topic until he had captured all of his thoughts related to it. In this manner, he saved details of information that might have otherwise slipped away and he constantly expanded his awareness. His illusion (view) of the world became more and more inclusive. In reviewing his rich experiences as an educator and life traveler, some new perspectives came into focus. He opened the new journal he had decided to keep and started writing.

* *

The early inhabitants of the earth lived mostly in lower and darker places. Travel was easier around lakes and streams. Food and water were in greater supply there. So was pestilence and disease. Ignorance and superstition prevailed. Little by little people learned things and made inventions that allowed them to venture onto higher ground and into higher levels of thinking. Employing slaves enabled a few people to live higher up and farther away from the bogs and bottoms. The invention of irrigation channels and aqueducts made it possible for more people to move outward and upward. Eventually humankind learned how to learn. They learned to collect information, analyze it, and draw conclusions. As they learned more, their living and learning expanded. This led them out of the darkness and away from superstition. They invented things that allowed them to travel far and wide on the surface of the earth. They invented things that let them communicate across great distances. They invented things that allowed them to fly higher than the highest places on the earth. One invention was paramount in this evolutionary process toward the light. It has been called the single greatest invention of modern man. It was the concept of reserved judgment, which became the basis of the scientific method. The scientific method has provided many benefits for mankind. In many cases, it has freed people from the limits of ignorance and superstition. However, science for economic profits has been given too much power in human affairs. In the ever accelerating rush into science-based *progress* a vital connection with the earth and its position in the universe has been lost. The active reverence that the ancients held for our home planet and its life giving star, the sun, is no longer prevalent. It has been largely replaced by aggressive pursuits of short-term personal gain with little consideration of how this affects the long-range future of life on the earth. Exploitation is not balanced with restoration and healing. This is a loss we might not recover from if we wait too long to recognize it and take corrective action.

Gautama Buddha taught that all views of the world are illusions. By that he meant that each person's view of the world is a selected picture of reality. Of the almost infinite number of things it is possible to be aware of, a person becoming acclimated to the world must select a very limited number to which they give their attention. If their limiting mechanisms went haywire and their senses were receptive to everything possible to attend to all at one time, they would probably "blow a fuse." The selection process is a potent tool for acceptance and survival. It can also be a powerful obstacle to growth and development. People can easily be trapped by limiting illusions.

In most cases, new lives are made secure in the world when they receive caring treatment from people in their groups of origin. As they experience such treatment they are taught by that experience. Their caregivers teach by everything they do in the presence of a developing person. The initiates are literally programmed to see the world as their teachers see it. They learn to see the good as whatever is included in their caregivers' views of what is good. Likewise with what is bad or threatening or dangerous. The particular illusion that is their window to the world reflects the norms of their primary group. One only has to travel from culture to culture to see how this varies in accordance with local selections. While a person can feel very comfortable with the fractional view of their home group it can severely limit their ability to see other dimensions outside those limits. It can also compromise their ability to cooperate with people who belong to other groups and have different programming.

For persons reared by alcoholics, drug addicts, or other dysfunctional caregivers, the programming they receive is a double whammy. What is learned while immersed in such a group teaches them things that have little constructive carryover to any situation outside their immediate home situation. Further, they learn to mistrust their own feelings and deny what their own senses tell them is taking place. They get programmed just like everybody else but with erroneous information. Their view of life is somewhat like the image in a single piece of a shattered fun house mirror. It is very limited. It is also grossly distorted.

* *

Gregg shuddered as he pondered the truth of these matters. He saw that he could have been imprisoned by his own experience and never have been aware of how it shut him down. He could have been accepted and nurtured into a world-view that no doubt would have been comfortable at the time. He could have been like the "nowhere man" the Beatles sang about and not have realized he was going round and round in a tight little circle. Irrelevant. A failed life experiment.

Finding a cosmic observation point

In 1971 NASA astronaut Dr. Edgar Mitchell climbed into his *Kittyhawk* command module and was blasted on a journey into outer space. He was the lunar module pilot of Apollo 14, NASA's third manned lunar landing. He was the sixth man to walk and work on the surface of the moon. It was an audacious time in the history of mankind. For Mitchell, however, the most extraordinary part of the journey was not kicking up moon dust. There was something else he did on that trip that grabbed Gregg's attention. He collaborated with two physicians to do some confidential research on telepathic communication. The three of them devised a plan that utilized research materials and techniques validated by the eminent paranormal research scientist, Dr. J. B. Rhine. They knew other researchers had found that the distance between two participants in this type of experiment had no effect on the results. And, the time between transmission and reception appeared to be instantaneous. They felt that Mitchell's trip offered an unparalleled opportunity to test whether telepathic communications could be transmitted over distances greater than those that could be measured on the earth.

The communicators in their experiment would be more than two hundred thousand miles apart. Mitchell and his collaborators saw their experiment as safe and non-intrusive. However, they knew that NASA administrators would not allow *any* deviations from approved procedures on a moon shot. They took an oath for absolute secrecy until after the results of their experiment were carefully analyzed. They agreed that if anything worthwhile was learned, it could be published when the extreme excitement surrounding a moon shot had diminished. They wanted to avoid contamination and distortion from news media desperate for eye-catching stories about such a momentous event.

The experiment was carried out on four separate evenings. There were two trials on the way to the moon and two more on the way back to earth. As the crew settled in for a try at sleeping in zero gravity, Mitchell quietly went to work according to the plan conceived before the launch. He took out a clipboard on which he had copied a table of random numbers and the five Zener symbols made popular by Dr. J. B. Rhine: square, circle, star, cross, and wavy line. He matched selected symbols with random numbers and organized the numbers with the random number table. He then concentrated on each matched symbol for fifteen seconds. Meanwhile, his collaborators back in Florida attempted to jot down the symbols in the same sequence he had arranged on his clipboard. Both he and his collaborators had a column of twenty-five spaces in which to write symbols during the time he was out in space. Each of these telepathic communication trials took about seven minutes. Then he zipped himself into his hammock for a few hours of sleep. The next "morning" he went back to the prescribed NASA routine without a second thought of the experiment.

The data collected in this experiment was carefully analyzed by Dr. J. B. Rhine in his laboratory at Duke University. Dr. Rhine also suggested that similar analysis be conducted elsewhere as an independent check. Another well-known researcher in the field, Dr. Karlis Otis, was selected to do this important work at his laboratory in New York. The results of the experiment, in terms of statistical probability, were profound. They strongly suggested that there was some kind of communication achieved that wasn't through any modes of conventional transmission. These findings made a significant impact on Gregg. They added powerful support to his growing awareness of the efficacy of telepathic communication. They added to the credibility of this mode of communication as an inherent ability of human beings. They corroborated his own personal experience in communicating telepathically with his friend Kate. Many times, over short distances of twenty or thirty miles. Once across the ocean, from Spain to the United States.

After Dr. Mitchell's audacious experiment Gregg found that there was increasing research into the nature of telepathic communication. In her book, <u>*Infinite Mind: The Science of Human Vibrations*</u>, Dr. Valerie Hunt describes telepathy as: "a kind of intuition---a direct knowing of distant facts devoid of time. The problem we mortals have in understanding the experience of knowing before things happen comes from our incomplete understanding of space-time. Einstein once commented that the distinction between past, present, and future is an illusion---although a stubborn one."

Since the publication of Mitchell's experiment, many other studies have validated the transfer of thought from one human mind to another across large distances and without normal time constraints. The results of these studies have been reported in several contemporary journals and books. In addition to Dr. Mitchell's <u>*The Way of The Explorer,*</u> another book that Gregg found most helpful in understanding telepathic communication was: <u>*The Conscious Universe: The Scientific Truth of Psychic Phenomena,*</u> by Dean Radin, Ph.D.

After extensive study of accumulating research data produced by credible scientists, Mitchell came to understand that all psychic phenomena are *energy* centered. He found that all of this information dealt with only two basic categories of psychic events: (1) where there is increased awareness of naturally occurring and man-made patterns of energy, and (2) where there is intentional (active) management of energy transformation processes. In his seminal book, *The Way of The Explorer,* he explained that:

> When an individual is quiet, relaxed, and receptive he/she can become more sensitive to and aware of the energy in the environment. Naturally gifted and/or well-trained people are more aware of the energy patterns from both internal and external sources than others. So the categories of telepathy, clairvoyance and the like just denote a greater awareness of naturally occurring and man-made patterns of energy. Intentionality is the active process of desiring or intending an action. Action requires the movement, or transformation of, energy---something each of us does everyday of our lives. Psychoactive people, either naturally or through training, have a greater range of actions they can intentionally and directly initiate with their mind.

Mitchell also observed that when these capabilities are utilized, they do not require moral and ethical considerations beyond those that apply to ordinary awareness and intentionality in everyday life. The nature of the energy involved is determined by its quantum mechanical qualities. "Like electricity, it can toast your bread or power an electric chair. It requires no special dispensation from supernatural authority. And it is precisely for this reason that virtually all the world's established esoteric traditions require practice of self-discipline and acquisition of spiritual values first, allowing the psychic capabilities to manifest when and if they naturally emerge. The idea here is to have a more compassionate and wiser individual in possession of such abilities." After his own experiment with telepathic communication and subsequent studies that led him to examine the entire range of related psychic abilities, Mitchell grew certain that these increased levels of psychic ability were "most likely latent, evolutionary and emergent in our species. But if our belief systems will not accommodate these natural abilities and they are suppressed early, they will not naturally emerge in the individual; there is just too much dogma in the way."

Mitchell's efforts "to reveal and interpret information, first in outer space, and now in inner space" quickly brought him into awareness that the existing division between science and religion stood in his way. For four hundred years, since the time of Rene Descartes, the church left science to the scientist and the scientist left religion to the theologian. That duality had more or less peacefully coexisted ever since. Mitchell realized that it must be resolved in order to answer his questions. He envisioned the new model of quantum mechanics as the key to integrating the religious and scientific realms of thought. He foresaw the reconciliation of these realms for understanding the universe simply because the findings of quantum mechanics research profoundly demonstrated their compatibility. He also came to believe that human beings must now assume a large measure of conscious control in their own evolutionary process because human volition was clearly a fundamental characteristic of nature.

The term Mitchell used to describe the profound change of perspective he experienced when he viewed the earth suspended in space was *epiphany*. Epiphany is the name for achieving intuitive insight. He said he experienced a *grand epiphany*. When Gregg read these words in Mitchell's book, he was reminded again of Paul Tillich's definition of revelation: that experience accumulates to a critical point and suddenly, *knowing* jumps to a higher level. The new perspective is greater than the sum of its parts. Mitchell said he became certain that experiencing epiphany is a latent possibility for every individual. "It is, to a large degree, what has allowed humankind to evolve in their thinking, as it brings about a sudden synthesis between existing ideas." From case studies reported by Richard Bucke in his book, *Cosmic Consciousness*, Mitchell said he learned that spontaneous epiphanies brought more than expansive awareness. They also provided a sense of inner peace, feelings of well being, and an unshakeable feeling of immortality accompanied by joy. He later found that modern psychiatrists and psychologists had noted similar results when individuals achieve reconciliation with sublimated and dissociated memories. Pain is released, healing takes place, and greater feelings of well-being and joy are experienced. He realized that in each situation a duality is healed. He believed that this is what happened to him out there in space on his way back from the moon. He felt a sense of unity and wholeness with the cosmos. The schism (duality) between his early religious upbringing and his later scientific training was suddenly resolved. It was a powerful and joyful gift from the Universal Mind.

Becoming aware of universal connections

When Edgar Mitchell returned from the moon, his life's direction changed dramatically. The overwhelming sense of universal *connectedness* stayed with him. He wrote that he saw more clearly how the traditional modes of understanding did not adequately explain modern day experience. He realized that most of our belief systems have been accumulated through external authorities rather than through our own quest and original insight. He saw that our beliefs were (and still are) in crisis. It was clear to him that the human community needed comprehensive revisions in their ideas concerning reality and truth. When he left NASA in the early 1970's, he founded the Institute of Noetic Sciences (IONS) in California. He wanted it to engage in scientific research that would ultimately help him better resolve the complex insights he gained from his experiences in space. His goal was to discover and then reveal more accurately and more fully the structure of reality as it was being experienced by "an emerging space-faring civilization." Mitchell saw his training as a jet pilot and astronaut somewhat incompatible with what was required of the modern-day shaman he felt himself becoming. He had always dealt with life in the present and in a concrete hands-on way.

He wanted to solve problems simply because they were there. As his attempts to understand his experience in space turned him inward, he tried to retain his scientific sensibilities. He became aware that his new life purpose was "to reveal and interpret information, first in outer space, and now in inner space."

Gregg found much in Mitchell's experiences of epiphany or revelation that correlated with his own. How he came to trust the process of serendipity as it occurred time after time in his life to provide him with opportunities to understand and choose. How he received information and guidance from the Universal Mind. He realized he would always be grateful to Edgar Mitchell for sharing his courageous explorations of outer and inner space. He was especially happy to learn about the location from which he viewed the earth and its place in the universe, the place Gregg now called *Mitchell's Point*. He once heard someone say that if you want to find four leaf clovers, a good place to look is in a clover patch. He was now convinced that an excellent place to look for joyful epiphanies and revelations is the visionary panorama one can find at *Mitchell's Point*.

Transcending ordinary perspectives

After he discovered Mitchell's Point, Gregg sent his perception out there many times. From that location he saw that even a life lived to old age is very short for each of us. Scrambling for a spot of earth and a collection of things that one can personally clutch to themselves for less than a hundred years is a kind of folly. A blip of geological time. A hardly noticeable ride through space like a shooting star. It is good to have a home and feel anchored somewhere. However, there is a lot more to life than that. If we grab, plunder, and trash, our children will have to live in fear no matter how much of the earth's resources we control during our own life span. A shortsighted result of illusions with dangerous limits. On the other hand, with more expanded and inclusive illusions, there can be opportunities to grow and learn.

People can enjoy their human life, however brief, and make positive connections as they cycle through time and space on their way to ultimate reunion with the creator of the Universal Mind.

Weighing the balance and finding hope

On one of his "trips" out to Mitchell's Point Gregg spent a long time thinking about the creative and productive powers of human beings. These soft little creatures, strung on a framework of fragile bones, have produced marvels of engineering and construction. Airplanes and automobiles and spacecraft. Dams and highways. Tall buildings with innards of steel. Blast furnaces and rolling mills. Tunnels under rivers and through mountains. Giant bridges. Skyscrapers. Telescopes anchored to the earth in isolated places. Telescopes and satellites and space stations that orbit the earth. Radios and microwave ovens. Television. Computers. Cell phones. Laptops. The world connecting internet. Besides the great admiration he had for airplanes, he could even get ecstatic over the underpasses and overpasses at the intersections of major highways. He saw them as gracefully soaring creations of art. Giant sculptures that bore great loads without complaint and sent each vehicle smoothly toward its chosen destination. While doing all of these physical and technical things, the species *Homo sapiens* also produced the Magna Carta and The Bill of Rights. They invented a government "of the people, by the people, and for the people" that they called democracy. They drafted the American Constitution. They created the World Bank and the World Court and The United Nations. They organized NATO and the European Union. They tied the world together with the Internet that spawned a myriad of tools and programs for social interconnecting. And they have started to develop ways for settling differences with diplomatic negotiations instead of the violence of war. So much accomplished during a relatively short tenure on the earth. And most of it during his own lifetime. He recognized that each advance had brought with it some serious problems. Pollution. Fragile controls on the unspeakable power of nuclear devices. Deadly waste products. Depletion of the Ozone layer. Unwitting disturbances of the ecological balance. Mind rot in the universal sedative of television. Unchecked gathering of power and wealth in the hands of a few addicted with an overwhelming urge to acquire and control. Rushing. Rushing. However, he observed that there was growing evidence that more and more people around the world are trying to understand these problems and support efforts toward creative resolutions.

CHAPTER VIII

At The Vertex

We are each on a journey to find ourselves. We are guided
in choosing pathways of action to not do harm, to repair
and restore what has been harmed, and to act in ways that
will add to the strength of our coming generations and the
world in which they will live. We must learn to walk softly
on Mother Earth and in the Cosmos.

---Frank Ettawageshik

Over the next several years Gregg found that he was increasingly
experiencing intuitive discoveries. Flashes of insight came while
he was meditating, driving, walking, running, or dreaming. They
came whenever his conscious mind was quiet enough to allow his
unconscious to be receptive. As he explored the meaning of these
experiences he was soon moved to reflect on how he arrived at
this potent juncture in his life. It all seemed to have a purpose. The
negative and positive events in his life inevitably led him here. The
negatives kept him from getting too settled in the usual and the
ordinary. The positives gave him opportunities to choose "the way
less traveled." Traveling in unknown territory, it was necessary to
watch where he stepped and where he camped for the night. Under
these circumstances, he developed an exceptional curiosity for
seeing beyond his own illusion and into the illusions of others. He
constantly searched for the universal ideas and principles that made
all illusions meaningful. The more he learned, the more he was

able to see. The more he was able to see, the more his illusion (view of the world) included. His new perspectives incorporated events and information experienced in the past with those of recent times. Time and locations didn't seem to matter. His awareness went from two and three dimensions to holographic. It was exciting. And, it was very rewarding. He was grateful for the learning opportunities. He often found his mind (perception) positioned out in space at Mitchell's Point. His view from out there grew exponentially larger and more inclusive. His perspective moved outward in ever expanding fashion from this imaginary vertex position. He saw the earth was a lustrous jewel among an infinite number of objects in the universe. He understood that all of the objects he perceived out there were marvelous manifestations of the Universal Mind. They were wondrous to behold. However, he saw that the needs of human beings would one day exceed the available resources and developing conditions on their home planet. He realized this would present enormous challenges. There would be many choices to make. He saw that the choices could be to respond in ways that were negative and destructive or in ways that were creative and productive.

Tuning in to the Universal Mind

He was never frightened by the insights he received through these channels. They did involve problems that he knew would require hard choices to resolve. Somehow he always *knew* that they were not cases of *fait accompli* and could be resolved by learning from and working *with* the Universal Mind. The insights didn't always arrive full-blown and fully developed. Often he was only able to hold on to key parts of the information received when it came in less impacting dreams. Sometimes a dream would be so powerful that it would abruptly wake him up and he would have no trouble recording it in vivid detail. Most of the time he received incomplete or partial information that required serious work to uncover the message it contained. His favored approach to deciphering these messages was to place himself in a hypnotic state. He would then give his inner mind permission to explore "anything and everything" that would help him to understand what the message was. When it began to come into focus, and he could put it into words, he would immediately try to share it with Jenna. She was a very good listener and could quickly identify the places in his thinking that were unclear and needed some more thoughtful work. She would patiently give him her attention. At dinner. While they walked. In the car. After lights out at bedtime. The latter was problematic in that his "melodic voice" sometimes lulled her back to sleep and he didn't get the benefit of her feedback on what he said.

His friend Kate was also very helpful in mining and expanding the information he had received. She always asked thoughtful and penetrating questions. She helped him make connections from what she knew about him, other information he had previously shared with her, reading she had done, her personal experiences, and her own seminal intuitions.

Through such exchanges with Jenna or Kate or both he was increasingly able to receive and understand information from the Universal Mind. When he was on a particular quest, it seemed that friends and colleagues sensed his need and spontaneously responded by sending him articles and calling his attention to relevant books. Sometimes he would have a strong urge to go to the bookstore and browse the shelves. To his amazement, just the right volumes seemed to be waiting for him. More than once he had the inexplicable experience of finding a certain book while browsing after a clerk had searched the store's computer files and told him they didn't carry it. Once a very timely book actually fell from a shelf and landed at his feet. It seemed that the more he accepted these events and was open to them, the more they happened.

In March of 1999, he participated in the third International Conference on *The Psychology of Consciousness, Energy Medicine, and Dynamic Change,* offered at Hilton Head Island, South Carolina, by The National Institute for the Clinical Application of Behavioral Medicine. At an all conference dinner meeting, he was seated at a large round table with seven other people. Five of the people were friends and others that he knew. One of the two strangers at the table was an obviously energized woman who offered to give psychic impressions to members while they were waiting for the speaker to start. She amazed and amused several people before she came to Gregg. When she made eye contact with him she hesitated briefly and then said, "you are a very spiritual person; one of the most spiritual people I have seen at this conference." He was surprised and pleased. As the speaker was being introduced, she passed him a note that said, "We need to talk. Please come out to the hallway after the speaker is finished." At the intermission, he followed her to a table across the hall. She repeated her earlier statement that she found him to be a very spiritual person. She said her ability to *see* such things was new in her life. It started happening around her fiftieth birthday (just as with the later Oracles of Delphi). She found she was able to see auras and instantly *know* a great deal about people. She was often aware of events before they happened. Also, she could visualize places and things far away. She said she was thrilled with these developments and was still learning how to handle them.

After some sharing of unusual and inexplicable experiences with each other, she told him she could see that he was already receiving information from the Universal Mind and was one of the people who would be helping to usher in a new era in human development. She also told him about a book, written by a British psychic and author named Alice Anne Parker that was an excellent resource for understanding dreams. The title of the book was <u>*Understand your dreams:1500 Basic Dream Images and How To Interpret Them.*</u> After the conference he purchased a copy of the book and found it immensely helpful. He felt this serendipitous meeting was truly one of synchronicity and that it gave another big boost to his spiritual development.

About this time he had a powerful dream in which he saw the biblical *Parable of The Talents* in a new light. The fundamental Christian preachers he had experienced early in his life often used it to threaten their parishioners. They presented God as a powerful patriarch who demanded that his people go forth in the world and do his bidding with the life he had given them. If they did not follow his command, he would be furious and punish them severely. It didn't square with Gregg's understanding of God as the source of all creation that is manifested in the world with love rather than jealous wrath and punishment. He had no trouble accepting that the parable was received from the Universal Mind. He also understood that it was filtered through the very limited perspective of the person who first received and recorded it. Those who laboriously hand copied this parable along with the rest of the Bible text during the superstitious and fearful Middle Ages probably found it quite fitting to see a dreadful message within it. Especially when great plagues were decimating the populations of Europe. The resulting versions of the parable were contaminated by the views of the translators and copiers that thought they were witnessing God's wrath. The fundamentalist preachers of Gregg's generation found in these versions powerful material for gaining adherence to their own creative views of the "gospel." However, he could see that they had grossly misinterpreted the parable to fit their own limited and fearful illusions of the world. From that perspective they thought there was a clear mandate in the verse of the parable that says, "Now then! Take the talent from him and give it to the one with ten. For to everyone who has, more will be given and he will grow rich; but from the one who has not, even what he has will be taken away." (Matthew: 28-29)

It was clear to him that the basic information from the Universal Mind, which the first receiver sought to communicate by writing the parable, was not about orders and threat and punishment. In the zeitgeist of a patriarchal society, with limited resources and devastating natural calamities, the concept of pleasing a jealous and wrathful father or suffering dire consequences was bound to contaminate any reflection on information received from that source.

He rewrote this verse of the parable to reflect what he had come to understand about the nature of the Universal Mind. "For anyone who pays attention and nurtures his/her connection to the riches (information) within the Universal Mind more access will be given, and he/she will be rewarded with ever greater awareness of his/her true relationship with God; but the one who does not use his ability to seek an ever-deeper connection to the Universal Mind will lose his/her ability to learn and grow *with* God." With that conflict (duality) resolved in his own mind, he felt the joy that comes with finding such resolutions. His epiphanic dream illuminated for him the unaffected meaning of the cosmic (universal) information on which the parable was based. It was actually about *opportunity. Opportunity to make choices* that could result in the evolution of human beings to new levels of creative and productive participation *with* God.

Thinking back to when the salamander appeared on the plastic grass at Uncle Ray's funeral, he *knew* it was no coincidence. Was it there to add another dimension to Uncle Ray's mysterious treasure story? Was it there to serve as a marker for Gregg's growing ability to be aware and "tune in" to the Universal Mind? Was there something in the survival story of its species that was critical to understanding what is needed for the survival of mankind? On the way home from the funeral, he told Jenna what he had seen and posed these questions. She listened patiently. He hoped she would come up with something to help him find the intended message. Nothing. Not a clue. However, they both knew that the search was very important and would be continued.

Many times over the next few years they discussed the possible message in the salamander's serendipitous appearance. The breakthrough came when Gregg followed the recommendations of a colleague and obtained a copy of Edgar Mitchell's _The Way of The Explorer._ His thought processes were kicked into overdrive by the discovery of Mitchell's insights on evolution and the future of mankind:

It has occurred to me that human destiny is still very uncertain, that the veneer of civilization is yet exceedingly thin. Believing as I do that the universe is intelligent, and understanding the absurd and tragic fate that awaits us, I have wondered whether or not we are prepared for our own survival, whether or not our own collective consciousness is yet high enough evolved. Our universe seems to learn by the blunt process of trial and error. But I now understand that we have a certain degree of control over the evolutionary process and can influence our own course. The only way to accomplish this is by bringing into question the very way we think about consciousness and the universe.

Finding the synchronized message of indigenous prophecies

Gregg first became aware of Dr. Alberto Villoldo in 2004, at an International Conference of the National Council on the Clinical Application of Behavioral Medicine. The unique qualities and experiences he presented in his workshop left Gregg with an urgent interest in pursuing a new line of information that transcended ordinary knowing. The theme of his workshop was taken from his seminal book, *The Dance of The Four Winds.* It chronicled his attempt to learn the healing secrets of the Peruvian shamans and correlate them with the basic tenets of Western psychotherapy. As he sat on the edge of a small stage in his assigned room at the conference, he said he had wanted to quickly learn from the shamans and then write a book that would make him a prominent expert in the psychology and anthropology communities of the western world. He had embarked on this quest expecting to learn what there was to know about the four paths of the Medicine Wheel in a year or so of intimate contact with the most respected shamans of Peru. It turned out be a journey that took him much longer than he anticipated.

He said that after he identified the most powerful and respected shamans, he naively set out to meet with them and quickly gain their cooperation for his project. After all, his plan was to share their wisdom in a way that would do much to establish their credibility. He reasoned that it was an opportunity for them to have a significant influence in the world at large. In addition, it would firmly establish him as a major contributor to the merging of the best of indigenous shamanistic healing methods with the best of western psychology. The dream soon proved to be more elusive than he imagined. Attempts to meet with shamans and discuss their methods were more often than not rebuffed or they yielded little of the information he sought. Little by little he did gain the confidence of some less powerful shamans. He participated in their ceremonies. He submitted to the use of mind-wrenching potions under their guidance. In this willing surrender to their care and processes, he learned enough to convince him that his quest was nevertheless valid and would yield worthwhile results in due time. However, he believed that engaging a certain well-known and very powerful shaman was critical to his mission. He had made many attempts to contact this man that did not have good results. A few times he had what he felt was a firm agreement to meet with this shaman at a designated jungle location. When he came on the scene, he only found the smoldering remains of a campfire or other evidence that someone had been there and recently departed. One day, after many such elusive and disappointing near misses, the shaman sent him a clear message to be at a certain jungle clearing where he would definitely be present.

When Alberto arrived at the designated place, the shaman was already there. He spoke first to the obviously eager young man, "I know who you are and I know what you want. Before we talk about that, I want you to do something. "Go over to the edge of the clearing. Walk ten steps into the jungle and stand there for about ten minutes. Then, come back here to where you are standing now." Alberto did as he was told. As he returned to the clearing, the shaman spoke again, "what happened when you went into the jungle?" "Not much, except that the usually noisy creatures that live there got very quiet." "Of course, they were aware of something that you need to know. The jungle creatures went quiet because they sensed that you have too much anger in your heart. When you can walk into the jungle and the creatures continue making their usual noises, come back to see me. You will then be ready for the things you want to learn." Alberto said he was greatly disappointed but gratefully accepted the challenge. However, achieving the readiness prescribed by the shaman took him more than eight years!

Gregg's encounter with Dr. Villoldo at the conference made an indelible impression. He bought and read several of his books over the next few years. When he learned that this fascinating scholar and explorer had established an experiential learning organization entitled, *The Four Winds Society, Inc.,* and was leading expeditions to travel with Peruvian shamans while experiencing sacred features of the Peruvian Andes, he was intrigued far beyond normal curiosity. He discussed this interest at length with his wife. She had long yearned see the ruins of Machu Picchu and said she would be happy to go with Gregg if the expedition included a visit to that mysterious site. During the summer of 2005, they signed on to an expedition labeled, "The Healer's Journey."

For eleven wonderful days they traveled with Dr. Villoldo and a special group of Inca shamans. They were said to be descendents of a group that evaded capture by the invading Spanish Conquistadores and had lived completely undetected high in the mountains until recent times. No one knew of their existence until one day a group of them simply appeared at a festival gathering. However, they were immediately recognized and heartily welcomed by those present at the festival. These diminutive and fascinating people let it be known that they were bearers of information critical to the well being of the earth that their ancestors had guarded and kept safe for hundreds of years. Also, they let it be known that they had decided to come down from their lofty isolation because they wanted to meet and talk with westerners so they could share this information. They said there was great need for it as the year 2012 approached. Contrary to the doomsday versions of the Mayan prophesy, they said the year 2012 would be a time of great change, but whether this change would be negative or positive depended on decisions that the earth dwellers chose to make in response to it. They said it could be a time of great opportunity to heal their relationship with Pacha Mama (Mother Earth) and create real peace in the world.

Gregg and his wife huffed and puffed as they were led beyond the ancient and high altitude city of Cusco. They climbed to even higher promontories and ancient temple ruins guided by the Inca shamans. Their lowlander lungs, not especially suited to steep climbing in the thinner air, were given a helpful boost by chewing coca leaves. These were abundantly provided by the shamans that understood the serious need of their visitors. The shamans were gentle and friendly, with profound wisdom acquired in direct connections with the Universal Mind rather than by the scientific methods of the western world. As the group walked the high trails to and from sacred sites, the shamans sensed the internal problems of their travel companions and offered personal healing treatments based on accumulated intuitive *knowing.*

Soon after returning to the United States from his profoundly illuminating experience in Peru, Gregg learned that certain tribes of American Indians had independently brought forth a prophesy for the year 2012 that synchronized neatly with the prophesy of the Inca shamans. The inherent message for earth dwellers was identical. It forecast a time of great change but the direction of the change would depend on the decisions and actions people made. He observed that there had been no direct communications between these indigenous groups. They were physically separated by thousands of miles. Yet they offered the same fundamental message. He felt the message was surely a gift from the Universal Mind. Two years later, his attention was called to the same basic message embedded in a book by Dr. Ravi Batra entitled, *The New Golden Age: The Coming Revolution Against Political Corruption and Economic Chaos.*

In conducting his insightful research in the field of economics, Dr. Batra identified certain cyclical regularities that had occurred in all cultures since the beginning of recorded history. On the basis of these findings, he predicted (prophesied) that in or near the year 2012 there would be great change in the world. Just like the Inca and American Indian prophesies had forecast. Based on his awareness of the cyclical regularities that he verified in his research, his prediction was that the great change forecast for the year 2012 would be the ending of the destructive features of an "acquisitive" cycle and was likely to be the beginning of a renaissance period he named "the new golden age." He said this change could be ushered in by the ballot box instead of violence. It would depend, he said, on what decisions people made.

It occurred to Gregg that the Universal Mind was the source of the message in all three of these prophesies, as well as the wrongly interpreted Mayan calendar inscription. The cyclical nature of such information could account for the regularities that are the basis of accurately timed prophesies. It also made contacts with it seem independent and unique even though they came through different channels and carried the same basic message from the Universal Mind. It was enough for him to firmly believe that the "tipping point" had been reached and that better times would be forthcoming.

Evolving spiritual intuitions and insights

Jenna was a supportive witness to Gregg's growing spirituality. For his birthday she bought him a "spirit house" she found on display at an art fair. It had a tripod frame about seventeen inches tall that held a variety of objects with spiritual significance. At the very top was a single tiny feather. There were no instructions for its use. Once purchased and/or given away, the meanings and powers invested were those created by the new owner. Choosing such an object for someone spoke volumes about how they were regarded. When he received the spirit house from Jenna he was overwhelmed with feelings of love and support. It also sanctioned their discussions of such esoteric topics as the spiritual meaning of a salamander appearing at a time and place where nobody expected it and the changing concept of evolution. After many explorations and trial positions, Gregg asked if they might set aside an evening to discuss and clarify his thinking on these topics. They agreed to go at it the following weekend. After dinner on Sunday, with some coffee and pecan pie to get them in a good receptive zone, they settled down to work. Jenna went first.

* *

"What you have been saying about evolution has really got me stirred up. How it conflicts with what I have been taught. The implications for the future of the world and human beings. I've been thinking about this constantly. I have some questions about this that I need answers to so I can reconcile some of my conflicting thoughts."

"Ask away. I'll do the best I can."

"O.K. Here goes. I was taught that God created the world and everything in it. Are you dismissing the idea of divine creation?"

"On the contrary. When I think of evolution, I don't see it in conflict with the idea that God created everything. I once had the experience of being in the audience when a panel of scientists at the University of Chicago presented the latest findings on the evolution of life in the world. Also in the audience were several Catholic Priests and Nuns. After the initial presentation, which outlined information to show the evolution of life from the hydrogen atom forward, one of the priests asked how this changed the concept of divine creation. The response was that it didn't. It only established an earlier beginning, with the creation of the hydrogen atom from which all the other elements and life eventually evolved. The reality of creation was not contested. Nothing in their scientific research disputed it. The date of creation was just moved back. Creation and evolution were both seen as God's handiwork. I was profoundly moved by that insight.

It was a whole new perspective. The discussion that followed, about how evolution worked, also had a big impact on me. Various factors could cause changes in the genes of living things that would result in changed characteristics in subsequent generations. I was especially fascinated by the fact that living things on the earth were constantly being bombarded by cosmic ray particles from elsewhere in the universe. And that these cosmic ray particles randomly collided with genetic material in living creatures, including human beings. Cosmic energy hits that dislodged minute parts of the genetic strand forever changed its makeup as a template for reproduction. These changes are most often too tiny to make a noticeable difference. When they accumulate, the sum total could make a significant difference. The concept of genes being altered by energy packets from outer space was fascinating and it had the ring of spiritual intervention."

"More of God's handiwork?"

"That's how I see it. We have learned there are lots of ways other than cosmic rays strikes that genes get changed. These include the effects of radiation, shortages of the right atomic parts, and even simple mistakes in replication. There is substantial evidence now on hand that the composition of matter and genetic changes (adaptations) can also be influenced by human thought."

"Are you saying that it is possible for human beings to manage the process of their own evolution? To choose the direction of their development and thereby increase their chances for survival of the species?"

"That's what Edgar Mitchell believes. And there is a lot of information gained from well conducted scientific studies to support him in that belief."

"That's a lot to swallow. It's hard to accept that you have been wrong or ignorant about something for most of your life."

"Thinking outside the box *is* difficult. It is even harder to change your way of doing something, even when you know that to continue doing it is harmful or will ultimately lead to disaster. If you have been doing it that way for a long time, it literally gets programmed into your unconscious mind and automatically resists being changed or discarded. That is a serious problem when you are presented with new information that proves something you learned earlier was wrong."

"O.K. Does this help you to know any more about the message in the salamander's appearance at your uncle's funeral?"

"I think it does. It's related to evolution. Something very important about evolution for human beings to be aware of. Also, I have learned that there is a powerful connection between diversity and evolution. The greater the pool of genetic differences in a given population, the more options for survival when the environment changes. Species that become too specialized are catastrophically vulnerable."

"Like the dinosaurs and the wooly mammoths?"

"Exactly. I recently read an article about a dinosaur discovery in the Sahara Desert that made me realize what the salamander's message might be. The monster *Jobaria Tiguidensis* was a Plant eating Sauropod. It was so perfectly designed for the world it lived in that it remained anatomically the same for millions of years. Other species around it had to heed the laws of natural selection through evolution to adapt to changing environments. But *Jobaria,* able to forage on the ground or rear up and chew the tops of trees, had a broad range of feeding possibilities. For millions of years it never needed to change and didn't. A different article said that the duckbilled platypus of modern times was another example of the fact that some animals remain the same for many millions of years. Twenty million years ago the platypus looked exactly the same as it does today. However, the encroachment of human beings into their habitats is pushing them toward the endangered species list. The salamander is a similar survivor. I think its appearance at Uncle Ray's funeral was a metaphor for something vital about evolution: *that sooner or later specialization (static sameness) is a one way ticket to extinction.*"

"Wow. That's quite a leap. But I think you might have something. I read an article myself the other day about how the development of hybrid crops has resulted in the kind of specialization that can make such crops vulnerable to extinction with the introduction of a new type of insect or a new variety of fungus."

"That's what I mean. A recent disastrous example is that some neighborhoods in Chicago planted only one type of shade tree and suffered massive losses with the influx of a tiny beetle that deprived those trees of the nutrients they required. Diversity in the population provides alternatives to prevent disaster when the environment changes. It can also provide a wide variety of resources for anticipating changes and getting ready to meet them."

"Amen. It seems so obvious now that we have it out on the table. And it's past our bedtime. I have a killer day tomorrow so I must get some sleep. But I'm glad we had this little talk. See you later."

She went upstairs to get ready for bed. He stayed awhile at the table where they had been talking. His adrenaline was up and his thoughts were still racing. He knew that it wouldn't be easy to gain acceptance for this information about evolution, especially if it was known how the salamander (that might have been a messenger from the Universal Mind) helped him discover it. Jenna's comment that it all seemed so obvious (to them) was certainly on target. He knew the information was not widespread in the conscious minds of the humans on the planet. Bringing it to their attention and getting it accepted as a basis for creative actions would be a formidable task. However, it was clear that people had been at such junctures many times throughout their tenure on the earth and many did choose to make creative and productive responses. Time to write! He picked up a pen and wrote in his journal until he had recorded all of his thoughts about what they had discussed.

* *

History is replete with examples of choices thought to be good, based on the information available at the time, only to find them terribly destructive later on as new information was discovered. A classic example is the use of tobacco products. For many years chewing and smoking tobacco was considered good recreation, even a special treat. Movie idols made it seem glamorous. Grandmas smoked corncob and stone pipes. Little children were "treated" to puffs from adults' cigarettes and taught how to inhale for the fun of it. A very large industry grew up around raising and processing tobacco. It was the backbone of early American agriculture. Then, it was learned that the use of tobacco was addictive and deadly.

At one time mercury was widely used in the manufacture of men's felt hats. A circle of wetted felt was smoothed down around a head-shaped wooden block. The felt covered block was then turned over and submerged into a tub of mercury. The pressure and fluid nature of the very dense mercury pressed the felt tightly to the shape of the block. It was a process that worked extremely well for forming hats. The mercury rolled off the hats and workers' hands as they were removed from the tubs. It was a "clean" and very effective operation. It was even fun to work with this mysterious metal. Then, it was discovered that mercury was very poisonous to breathe or touch. People who had worked on the production lines for many years without concern developed incurable illnesses from the mercury that got into their bodies through their lungs or the skin on their hands.

When it was found that radium could be used to make paint that would glow in the dark entrepreneurs quickly adapted this new technology to the manufacture of watches. The numerals on the dials of watches were painted with radium paint so they could be seen at night. It was a wonderful innovation that consumers loved. Everybody wanted one. Lots of people retired their old watch and bought a new one that mysteriously glowed in the dark. Many went to work in watch factories to meet the demand. It was job that called for precision placement of tiny amounts of the special new paint. Hundreds of times each day the painters wiped their delicate brushes with a cloth and then wet them in their mouths to shape a tip sharp enough for the job. Many years went by before it was discovered that the benign looking radium paint glowed because it was radioactive and the radioactivity was slowly killing the hapless painters.

Until the late 1950's it was common to have carbon tetrachloride fire extinguishers in many American homes. When the clear liquid was sprayed on a fire it would quickly exhaust the oxygen supply that effectively stopped the burning. Carbon tetrachloride was also used around the house as a cleaning fluid. It would cleanly dissolve oily spots on clothing and other fabrics. It seemed to be a friendly and reliable substance for use in the home. Then, it was discovered that the heat of a fire caused the harmless carbon tetrachloride to change into phosgene gas that was deadly to human beings who breathed it. After that discovery the carbon tetrachloride fire extinguishers were removed from the market.

Cocaine in Coca Cola. Using a fluoroscope to examine people's feet in shoe stores. Hydrogenated oils. Saturated fats. Getting burned in the sun. Using asbestos for insulation. DDT. There are many other examples of things in our environment we once valued highly and then wisely changed our assessment. Based on the evidence we had when they were introduced our previous views made good sense. Later, with new information we saw them in a different way and changed our perspective. It didn't make sense to see them in the old way anymore.

Scientific studies tell us that the star we call the sun has a finite life span. Although it is expected to shine for another five billion years, it is at least halfway through its estimated life. As the sun dies it will become an immense *red giant* engulfing the inner planets and scorching the earth. It will eventually exhaust its fuel supply and become extinct. Long before its death as a star, it will probably behave in convulsive ways that will not support human life as we now know it on the earth. While that is a very long way down the road, it is not forever.

Deposits of coal and other fossil evidence in Antarctica indicate that tropical conditions once existed there. In other words, the earth shifted it axis of rotation at some time in the past. Little is known about how or why this change occurred. One theory suggests there might have been sudden movement of molten material under the tectonic plates of the earth's crust that caused a change in axial orientation. Another theory suggests that a glancing hit by a mega meteor might have caused the shift. Whatever the reason for the change, the fact that it happened before is reason to believe that it could happen again. How soon this might happen is currently a deep mystery. One thing is certain, if and when it happens again human beings will be faced with enormous survival challenges.

In the meantime, there is the possibility that our earth will be on a collision course with lesser meteoroids or other space debris. They might not be powerful enough to change the earth's angle of axial rotation, but long before the sun plays its violent swan song such events could once again create the kind of environmental changes that extinguished the dinosaurs and wooly mammoths.

Just as it is with an individual human life, there is no guarantee of tomorrow. The forces of nature may allow folks on the earth anywhere from a few days to several billion years to prepare for such catastrophic changes. Under these conditions, *Homo sapiens* could be the ultimate endangered species.

All of the information needed for developing effective survival strategies is within the universal energy field. By seeking help from the Universal Mind, *Homo sapiens* "can do this." The time to educate everyone to the macro-reality of the human situation is now. The need to turn human attention toward development of the technological and spiritual attributes required for living elsewhere or in some other way is imminent.

* *

He closed his journal and headed for bed himself, hoping to sleep and dream some more.

CHAPTER IX

A Treasure Found

> There is one thing stronger than all the armies in the world
> and that is an idea whose time has come.
>
> ---Victor Hugo

The clock on the dresser said 3:12 a.m. The house was quiet as a tomb. Jenna was beside him in the big brass bed they bought after listening to Bob Dylan sing *Lay Lady Lay* a thousand times. She was sleeping peacefully. She only moved a little when he sat up with a start at the end of his dream. He felt totally awake. His breathing was more rapid than normal. He could feel the adrenaline coursing through his system. He knew something very special had happened.

It was one of those dreams that felt so real he wondered if he were awake or asleep. He had experienced many dreams of this type before. He was reassured when he saw that the clock said 3:12 a.m. because he knew that this type of dream typically occurs around this early morning hour. He had learned to work with such dreams so he could discover the messages they contained. Lay still. Don't turn over or you'll turn it off. Observe everything in it and fix each thing in your mind so you can remember it when you wake up. Think about what the message might be. When you have as much as you can extract, get up and record everything you can as soon as possible. Write it. Or tape it. Repeat the scenes over and over in your mind. Try to keep it all fresh and alive. Keep a part of your mind working on it until the insight comes. Sometimes it comes right away. Sometimes it takes a few hours. Sometimes it takes several days of trial and error ruminating. When it does come into focus you will know for sure what is the message embedded in the dream.

He expected that Jenna would understand his dream experience and have some helpful ideas about what the message might be. Her intuitions were on target more often than not. She had intimate knowledge of his life story and personal issues. She had helped him decipher many of his dreams in the past. He wanted to wake her and get at the heart of this one as soon as possible. He also knew that she needed to continue sleeping. She had a very demanding day ahead of her when the alarm went off at 5:30 a.m. She would be rushing to get ready for the day's events while he prepared breakfast. It was not the time to interrupt her tight routine and introduce such a momentous subject. He would wait until after dinner so he could have her full attention. He quietly got out of bed and went down to the home office they shared. All around the room friendly little green lights signaled that the computer, printer, copier, fax machine, telephone, and answering machine were ready to help him process information. It was a good place to think and record things so they could be studied and understood.

Receiving a special gift from the Universal Mind

He loaded a microcassette into the little battery-powered recorder and began to talk about what he had experienced. When it was all on tape, he played it back slowly and typed everything into the computer. All the while he tried to distance himself from it a little and feel what the message was. There were two scenarios. In each there was a great deal of tearing down with the aim of rebuilding. In one scenario vibrating power was used and a lot of old structures not planned for demolition were inadvertently destroyed. He was apprehensive that the people who used the vibrations to initiate changes were not completely trustworthy. They used power they didn't fully understand or know how to use safely. They represented their work falsely, made destructive errors, and took advantage of their constituents. In the other scenario previous remodeling efforts were found to be cosmetic cover-ups. Close inspection revealed that there were worn out infrastructures and decaying foundations. They, too, were demolished. In each situation it was clear that replacement was to be fundamentally new, not made over.

Gregg's talk with Jenna that evening left them both feeling that this was the most important dream they had ever discussed. But how? The fundamental message eluded them. They agreed to let their inner minds work on it for a while and trusted that helpful insights would eventually arrive to help them understand. Over the next several weeks Gregg slowly came to realize that he was experiencing a revelation. Information was coming in from the Universal Mind like email messages on his computer. It accumulated steadily. Then something happened! It was like looking at a holographic image from a different viewpoint and discovering another image imbedded within the first. Information that was there all the time and unseen suddenly became prominent. Foreground yielded to background. A hidden treasure was found!

It was about 10:00 a.m. on a Tuesday morning. He was alone in the house. He needed to talk about what had happened. He reached for the phone and dialed Kate's number, She didn't answer so he left a message.

"Please call me back as soon as you can. I have something very special to discuss with you."

He went downstairs and put the kettle on the stove to make some tea. He half-heartedly looked in the refrigerator and cabinets for some kind of snack. The kettle whistle seemed more piercing than usual. He resented the intrusion into the quiet space where he was examining the treasure and moved quickly to separate the kettle from the heat. The noise stopped at once. He poured the hot water into his cup and started the tea to brewing. When it was finished he moved to the table and went back to thinking about the treasure. He hoped Kate would call back soon.

At 11:15 a.m. the phone rang.

"Gregg, This is Kate."

"Hi. Thanks for calling back."

"You sound excited."

"I was! I am! I found a treasure!"

"What do you mean you found a treasure?"

"I had a really special dream."

"You're always having special dreams. What is so really special about this one?"

"It's not just a dream about personal stuff. It's something really important for everybody. I had a dream about 3 weeks ago. I've been working on it ever since. It was about tearing down old things to replace them with something new, not made over. Little by little the big picture has been coming into focus. This morning I hit the jackpot!"

"Is it about gambling?"

"No! It's about group dynamics."

"Group what?"

"Group dynamics. The unwritten principles that govern relationships of people in groups."

"O.K., I'm listening."

"Whenever two or more people form a group, there are universal principles that apply to their relationships in that group and with others who are not members of their group. These principles exist and they are in constant operation whether or not people are aware of them. In a way they are like microwaves. They exist and they operate in certain predictable ways. Yet they are not visible to the human eye. Just their effects. Learn what they are and how they work and you can use them for enormous benefits. Let your ignorance put you in their path at the wrong time and the wrong way and they'll do you great harm."

"You are losing me. Relationships in groups. Microwaves. What does all this mean?"

"It means that ever since the days of Cain and Abel human beings have been making a colossal error that has wasted enormous resources and cost many millions of lives because they unwittingly invoked destructive attributes of the basic principles of group dynamics. If people can learn about these principles and adjust their actions accordingly the world can be a much better place."

"What are these principles?"

"Well, I *know* what they are and I'm still working on how to state them in words that are easy to understand. I would like to get together for lunch or something sometime soon so we could work on this together."

"Sure. How about tomorrow? At the teahouse in the Japanese Garden? About noon?"

"Great. Thanks. I really appreciate it."

He was elated that he and Kate would be getting together so soon. She had a way of asking questions that really helped him to clarify his thoughts. Her questions were drawn from her own intuitions. Once the subject matter was identified it seemed that she could tune in to the same information he was receiving. She would reframe it into just the right questions to get his thought processes flowing. They had teamed up like this to examine many important subjects over the past eighteen years. He was truly grateful for the privilege of knowing her and having access to her inside track with the Universal Mind. He started working on the drafts they would discuss the next day at the teahouse.

Gregg wanted to write the Principles of Group Dynamics with powerful clarity and simplicity that would command attention. Unfortunately, the information came to him in a form other than language. He knew what the principles were. They seemed so clear in his thoughts and he could feel their power. When he tried to translate these thoughts and feelings into words the clarity and power disappeared. He worked on them all afternoon. Writing them out until each of the concepts was fully stated. Trying different words to say more succinctly what was needed. Trying various combinations to reduce the number of statements so each would speak with more power. He felt it was somewhat like trying to find and fit pieces into a complex jigsaw puzzle. Lots of trial and error. Lots of almost fits. He wanted the exact fit that would help to create a picture that would capture everyone's attention. He decided to bring the last draft of eight lengthy statements to his meeting with Kate the next day. If he could help her understand the principles, he felt certain that she could help him find better ways to state them.

The Teahouse was busier than usual. The noise level was too high for easy conversation. They decided to have lunch first and then find a quiet place outside where they could talk. It was a gorgeous day. The sun was filtering through the green forest canopy to speckle the ponds and plantings with rays of white/gold. As they passed by a tranquil pond a great white carp appeared at the surface and watched them in anticipation. Maybe that old fish thought they were bringing him something good to eat. On the far side of the pond was a small clearing with a nice shady bench. To get there they had to cross an arched wooden bridge over the little creek that flowed leisurely into the eastern end of the pond. The location gave them the privacy of distance with a clear view of the only path that led to where they were sitting. Gregg got out his drafts and read them to her. She listened intently and made some notes on a pad she had pulled from her pocket.

"Human beings come together to form groups in order to meet a basic need for togetherness. They want a sense of safety, of being loved, and of being valued by others. When they get together and interact with each other there are principles that apply to the dynamics of their relationships within the group as well as between their group and others. These are the *principles of group dynamics* that I (re) discovered in my dream. Here is how I have stated them at this time:

1. Interaction tends to induce sentiments of liking among those who interact.

2. Among those who interact, sentiments of liking for each other tend to increase as the frequency of interaction increases.

3. Where there is frequent successful interaction, there are positive benefits to those interacting.

4. Groups with a history of frequent interaction develop rules or norms for acceptable behavior toward others in the group.

5. Where there is frequent interaction the positive benefits cause members to value their membership in a group.

6. Members that prize their membership in a group adjust their behavior to comply with the rules or norms of that group.

7. When members value their membership in a group and choose to interact within its boundaries, there is an increase in exclusive and excluding actions by the members.

8. Exclusive and excluding actions by members of cohesive groups reflect their value judgments that are inadvertently felt as negative and hostile by other groups.

"Well, they seem to hang together and make a lot of sense. I do have some questions."

"I thought you might. I was hoping you would."

"OK. What do you mean by interaction? I think I know but I'm not sure that what I'm thinking is what you mean."

"Good question. You always ask good questions. Interaction in this case means the *exchange* of important information. Not just doing things together or being around each other. Exchanging information with each other that is important to both parties. It can be about any topic that is meaningful to both of them. For diehard baseball fans, it can be about baseball. For fishermen, it can be about fishing. For high school sports teams, it can be about the games. For members of an organized religion, it can be about their faith. For members of an extended family or ethnic group, it can be about the who, what, and where of their members' activities."

"So the term interaction as used in the first principle means the exchange of important information with others. Just being in the presence of others or even part of the same community isn't enough."

"Correct."

"Help me understand what you mean by sentiment of liking."

"Sentiment of liking means that if you and I exchange information with each other that is important to both of us, we will tend to think positive thoughts about each other. This will increase as the frequency of our interaction increases. In other words, the more often we exchange important information with each other the more we will tend to appreciate and like each other."

"In your third statement you say that where there is frequent interaction there are positive benefits to those interacting. In this context, what does the term benefits mean? What are some of the benefits? How does one get these benefits?"

"Well, a benefit is anything that promotes the welfare or improves the state of a person or group. In this context it is whatever the interacting persons gain as a result of their frequent interaction. A sense of belonging. Friends to do things with. Stimulation. Learning that promotes personal growth. Protection. Help to do things one can't do alone. Inside information. Economic advantage. Collective power."

"OK. In statement number four you say that members who value their membership in a group develop rules or norms for acceptable behavior toward others in the group. How do they do that? Are they aware of it when they are doing it? I've been in lots of groups and I didn't see any rules or norms in writing anywhere. Nobody talked about them. Are rules and norms interchangeable? Do they mean the same thing?"

"Well, a rule is an authoritative regulation governing conduct, action, procedure, arrangement, etc. And a norm is a rule that has become a designated standard, or model, or pattern of average behavior in a group. In interacting groups such rules or norms arise inadvertently out of the frequent interaction by the members.

Members aren't able to see them or say what they are, but they feel them and don't go far beyond the limits they set. They just *know* what they can and can't do if they want to keep their membership in the group. It's a little like the invisible electric fence my neighbor has for his dog. The dog knows here the boundaries are. He also knows he will be in a lot of trouble if he tries to go outside them."

"Invisible, yet very influential."

"Absolutely. Also, statement number five says that where there is frequent interaction the positive benefits cause members to value their membership in a group. And statement number six says that members who value their membership in a group will adjust their behavior to comply with the rules or norms of their group."

"Do you mean that people will unconsciously let the group they belong to tell them how to behave?"

"That's what the research shows. And there will be hell to pay if they don't. Even if the rules are not in writing anywhere, they know what they are. Little by little their experience in the group teaches them what the rules are and what happens when they are violated."

"You know, Gregg, so far these statements are interesting and they make sense to me. But I don't see what you were so excited about. Where the power comes from. They seem rather benign to me."

"We're getting to that. We're heading upstream to where the treasure is hidden."

"OK. I think I understand what you have explained so far. INTERACTION LEADS TO SENTIMENT AND SENTIMENT LEADS TO NORMS. NORMS ARE UNWRITTEN RULES WHICH CONTROL BEHAVIOR IN GOUPS. How does this lead to the treasure?"

"Well, statement number seven says that when members value their membership in a group and choose to interact within its boundaries, there is an increase in exclusive and excluding actions by the members. They like their group a lot because it meets their needs. They get connectedness and support from their interaction in it. It is a source of enjoyment. They see it as a great group. They decide they would rather belong to this group than any other. They do most of their interacting within the confines of this group. They see it as the best group. Their membership is a big part of their identity. In the short run this is wonderful. In the long run, it collides with a fundamental law of group dynamics. This law is found in statement seven which also says that exclusive and excluding actions by members of a cohesive group reflect their value judgments which are inevitably felt as negative and hostile by other groups."

"Wow! This means that when groups are exclusive and excluding they unwittingly set up conditions that will lead to hostility and hatred from other groups. They don't have to do anything to these groups to incur their wrath. Just choose their own group as the best. Or refer to their group as superior and favored by God."

"There you have it. These principles and the correlated law of group dynamics are the treasure I (re)discovered in my dreams. This treasure has been hidden away like treasures usually are. Others have discovered all or part of it over the past two thousand years only to lose it or see it deliberately hidden away again. The *power* is in the knowing about the principles and how they work. Then the negative and destructive consequences of invoking the law can be avoided."

"You say that others have previously discovered all or part of this treasure and then it was hidden away again. Who are some of these others?"

"Well, this treasure is actually information within the Universal Mind. In recent times three people that I know of somehow tuned in to this information: George Homans, Erich Fromm, and Regina Schwartz. It profoundly influenced their thinking and inspired new perspectives on human relationships. Each of them wrote outstanding books that included this information although they did not specifically identify the *principles or correlated law of group dynamics* in the way that they have been revealed to me now. It was the intuitive work of these people that provided the basis for the revelation I received. It happened just like the theologian, Paul Tillich, reasoned that it would. Information kept accumulating and accumulating until (voila!) it coalesced into a new perspective that included and transcended it all. Suddenly, the whole became greater than the sum of the parts."

"So you think these folks got very close and what they wrote gave important clues as to where the treasure was located."

"Right on! It was like finding gold dust and nuggets in alluvial deposits downstream from the mother lode. I think Regina Schwartz even found a major vein where a lot of the dust and nuggets came from. Follow the drift and deposits upstream. Find the vein she described. Let those clues help you decipher where to dig for the real treasure."

"I've heard of Erich Fromm and I read his book *The Art of Loving*, a long time ago. I thought it was a great book. I don't recall anything about group dynamics in that book. Did I miss it? Or was the group stuff in other books he wrote?"

"The book where he deals with group dynamics was entitled *The Sane Society.* It was published in 1955. In this book he discussed the basic needs of all human beings and how they can be satisfied. He was a highly regarded therapist and researcher in the field of mental health. His experience and intuitions led him to identify basic needs of all human beings if they were to have good mental health. One of these needs was for connectedness; a sense of belonging. Dr. Fromm said that this need could be satisfied in ways that were either healthy or unhealthy. The healthy ways were those that resulted in ever expanding ties with humanity. The unhealthy ways were those that were exclusive and excluding."

"In other words he was aware of most of the information that you now see as the principles and correlated law of group dynamics. He interpreted this in terms of mental health and realized there would be problems if the need for connectedness was satisfied in ways that were exclusive and excluding."

"Yes. I was really fascinated by his insights. I thought about them a lot. I referred to them in several papers I wrote in graduate school. They occupied an indelible place in my mind. I never let go of them. I knew they were very special even though they didn't seem to have a very big impact on the public at large. For me, they formed a fundamental resource for learning about and understanding what happened in human affairs."

"You said there were three people. Who were the other two?"

"Well, you probably never heard of George Homans. He wrote a very complex and powerful book entitled: *The Human Group.* It was first published n 1951. Dr. Homans was educated at Harvard. He later joined the Harvard faculty in their new Department of Social Psychology where he tried to follow his intuitions and be academically correct. He was a courageous explorer who tried to do ground breaking research yet stay within the bounds of institutional propriety. For more than 20 years he studied and wrote about life in small groups. He identified and refined the concepts of interaction, sentiment, and group norms. From his studies he learned that cohesive groups generate feelings of hostility toward other groups and elicit hostile feelings from other groups as a result of their cohesiveness. I applied this information to the management of classroom behavior and taught it to many prospective teachers. Even though I completely missed the principles of group dynamics on which it was based, Homan's work had a big impact on me. Just like Fromm's did."

"So, information was accumulating that would lead you to find the principles that eventually led to discovering the law."

"Exactly. The writer whose work was the catalyst for the revelation I am struggling with now was Regina Schwartz. She wrote a superb book that was published in 1997. She called it *The Curse of Cain.* When I heard about it I knew it was really special. When I read it I was just blown away. It took great integrity and a lot of courage to write such a book because it contradicted a lot of conventional dogma. She was teaching the Bible to undergraduates at Northwestern University when a student asked a question that punched a big hole in what she had been telling them about Jewish history. She said she had to write an entire book to answer his question. Her research for this led her to identify a principle of scarcity that pervades most thinking about identity. She also saw how such thinking results in exclusive and excluding behavior by insiders of a cohesive group. She offered many examples of how the impulse to define, limit, and possess had led to violence throughout history."

"How did you get from there to the principles and the law?"

"My dream! My really special dream! It all came together in my dream! After reading Dr. Schwartz's book I couldn't quit thinking about it. Awake or asleep. Actually, I had several dreams that kept moving in that direction. Then came the big one. And then the real breakthrough on Monday morning when I called you."

"So, what you meant when you said you (re)discovered these principles and the law was that you got there by following the trails blazed by Erich Fromm, George Homans, and Regina Schwartz."

"That's true. These thoughtful searchers for the truth were the trail blazers for me. They probably aren't the only ones who came so close to the treasure. It just might be that when Jesus of Nazareth told his followers to love their neighbors as themselves he was in touch with the information in the Universal Mind on which the principles are based. I didn't create them. I just happened to be tuned into the right frequency and they came bounding into my awareness."

"Now I see what you were excited about. The power of these principles and the law is starting to come through. The more I think about them, the more they seem to expand. And examples are coming in from all directions that illustrate what happened when they were not taken into account. Ugh! What a terrible waste!"

After their meeting Gregg let it all rest for a while. He told himself that it would be helpful to let things "perk" for several days before he tried to rewrite the principles and the law. On the following Sunday afternoon he felt like it was time to have at it. The resting had helped. Three hours later he had revised the seven statements into four:

1. Interaction among members of a group tends to induce sentiments of liking that increase as the frequency of interaction increases.

2. Where there is frequent interaction, there tends to be positive benefits to those who are interacting that cause members to value their membership in a group.

3. Groups with a history of frequent interaction tend to develop rules or norms for what is acceptable behavior toward others in the group, and members who value their membership in a group adjust their behavior to comply with the rules or norms for that group.

4. When members of a group selectively choose to interact within its boundaries, there is an increase in exclusive and excluding actions that invoke a universal law correlated with the principles of group dynamics: *exclusive and excluding actions will be felt as hostile and generate hostile responses by others, which ultimately will cause the ingroup to be attacked by outsiders.*

Later that evening, he asked Jenna if she would review the new versions and share her thoughts. She looked them over carefully and said she thought they were fine as written when accompanied by explanations of the terms. Then she went off to bed. He put the statements in a folder and laid the folder on top of his in-basket. "I'll fax these to Kate tomorrow," he thought to himself. Almost a week went by before he called Kate to say he was ready to discuss the revised versions of the principles. She agreed with the briefer format. She felt the principles and the law were clearly and concisely stated. She also agreed with Jenna that they should be accompanied by a subtext of specific definitions for the terms interaction, sentiment, norms, and benefits. He knew that she had given this a lot of thought. Her approach to evaluating other things he had written was to place herself in the position of prospective readers. She tried to imagine what message came through to someone reading it for the first time. He was sure she had tried to do that with these statements of the principles. At the same time, he wondered if her ability to do so was in any way compromised by her intimate involvement in their development.

With a good working draft of the principles and the correlated law of group dynamics now in hand, he was suddenly released from the feelings of extreme urgency that had been with him for so long. They might need to be dressed up a little but they were essentially ready for publication. He would get professional help with the fine-tuning of the printed words and plan how to make this information available to the world at large. He felt like a midwife about to assist in an imminent birth. His imagination put him to work "boiling the water and tearing the sheets" needed for the birthing process.

Inspired help that served as a catalyst

He was thinking about where to go from this threshold position when his office phone started ringing. He was surprised to hear Jenna's voice. She was calling from the cell phone in their car. The timing was perfect and surely it was no coincidence. She had been thinking constantly about the principles and what she had to say made him realize that something very important about them was not yet expressed. She agreed that when definitions for the terms were included the principles were clearly and concisely stated. She also felt that this format was too academic and mechanical. It seemed cool and detached, like a good lab report. As such, there wasn't enough attention to the relationship of the principles to the humane and loving outcomes that would motivate people to accept them and put them to use. As she talked he realized that both she and Kate had previously expressed some feelings about this deficiency. In his push to get the principles and the law written clearly and concisely he had chosen not to hear or explore what they were feeling. He was grateful for Jenna's comments at this time because they effectively slowed him down and gave him an opportunity to revisit the issue.

After their phone conversation he struggled with how to add the needed information to what he had written about the principles and the correlated law. Erich Fromm's insightful book *The Art of Loving* suddenly reappeared in a flash of insight. He realized that the premises of this book were analogous to what he wanted to say about the principles of group dynamics. According to Dr. Fromm, most people sincerely want to love and be loved. The potential for loving is naturally endowed. The ability to activate that potential may be undetected or even repressed by negative environmental circumstances. He proposed that developing this ability is like learning to be an artist. One must first learn the tools of the art and then use them to practice, practice, practice. He further stated that the practice of any art has certain general requirements, regardless of whether we are dealing with the art of carpentry, medicine, or the art of loving. Effective practice requires discipline, concentration, patience and supreme concern with mastery of the art. Such practice may be academic and rather mechanical at the start. Properly using the tools over and over again in the service of the art can result in experiential learning that eventually transcends the academic and mechanical. Intuition and feelings gradually take the lead in how the tools are used. The evolved result is a kind of metamorphosis: from competent practitioner to genuine artist.

Gregg realized that the principles of group dynamics can be used as tools for developing positive and productive relations in and between human groups. While the use of these principles as tools may be academic and mechanical at first, positive results may be obtained through their application "by the book." It was clear to him that the application of these principles is open to individual purpose, skill, and creative abilities. Diligent practice at applying these principles with *supreme* concern for mastery of the art can lead to creative and transcendent expressions. At this level, the art of applying the principles of group dynamics may be utilized for avoiding hostility and violence in human affairs. It can also enable groups to work together under conditions that offer each and every member safety, affection, a sense of value, and the genuine love that is manifest in the Universal Mind.

He *knew* that his efforts to understand and articulate this information were being gently guided by the Universal Mind. The strong support he received from Jenna and Kate had greatly helped him to learn from his mystical experiences. However, he still felt somewhat vulnerable when he thought of sharing the principles and the law with others. That feeling changed when he read *Reinventing Medicine* by Larry Dossey, M.D. A research report cited in that scientifically sound and inspirational book provided significant validation for people who had spiritual and mystical experiences:

> Surveys by the University of Chicago's National Opinion Research Council (NORC) find that 'people who have tasted the paranormal, whether they accept it or not, are anything but religious nuts or psychiatric cases. They are for the most part, ordinary Americans, somewhat *above* the norm in education and intelligence and somewhat *less* than average in religious involvement.' Sociologist Andrew Greely of NORC tested people who had profoundly mystical experiences, such as being bathed in white light. When these persons were subjected to standard tests measuring psychological well-being, the mystics scored *at the top*. University of Chicago psychologist Norman Bradburn, who developed the test, said no other factor had ever been found to correlate so highly with psychological balance as did mystical experience.

Reading that information lifted him to a new level of readiness for sharing what he had learned. It was past midnight. The house was quiet. He was alone in their home office. So many ideas were still coming together; coalescing into new perspectives. Too energized to sleep, he decided to put some more of his thoughts in writing. He expected that Jenna would soon be asking him more questions about the principles. She would be thinking of what was important for helping others to understand and make good use of them. Anticipating what she would ask and writing what might be required to answer her thoughtful questions would use up the excess adrenaline in his system. He knew from past experience that sleep would come easily after that was done. He picked up a pen and started writing.

* *

When Uncle Ray told his stories about a mysterious lost treasure, he always made it sound as if it were more valuable than any treasure we had ever heard about before. He said we could find it if we tried hard enough. It always seemed as if it were not far away. When we had begged for more clues he told us to think about it often and one day, when we were ready, we would find all of the clues we needed. Now it is clear that the treasure is to be found within. When somebody is ready to look within to where they can connect with the Universal Mind. The treasure available through that connection is *information.* Uncle Ray must have known about this connection. Whatever he might have learned from it himself probably wouldn't have brought him much positive recognition from his community at that time. By encoding his awareness in mystery stories he was able to make it available to anyone who might later develop the ability to tune in and understand. The spirit (treasure) of Uncle Ray was not lost after all. His physical body was carefully secured in a steel casket inside a concrete vault and buried in the ground. However, the energy (information) of his spiritual essence was not confined there. It returned to the cosmos where it is available to others who are ready to tune in and grow *with* the Universal Mind.

The principles of group dynamics and the correlated law apply across the entire human population. It is clear that whenever two or more people form a group there can be real benefits. At the same time there will be consequences arising from their togetherness. As the group grows stronger and more beneficial to its members, they will naturally place more value on their membership. Assessing the options and choosing to belong to a particular group is a selective activity. When more value is placed on one group, less value is given to the groups not chosen. It is an exclusive and excluding process. Those who are insiders have an exclusive relationship. Those who are outsiders are excluded.

The more a group engages in exclusive and excluding activity, the more they will generate feelings of hostility toward other groups and the more other groups will feel hostility toward them. In other words, when people are successful in making choices and create an exclusive and excluding group, they also set in motion forces that will ultimately cause them to be attacked from without. This sad state of affairs has been repeated time and time again since the time of Cain and Abel.

In her book *The Curse of Cain,* Regina Schwartz documents adherence to a principle of scarcity that has been the classic basis for making exclusive and excluding choices. This principle points to limited property held by a father who must choose only one heir because there isn't enough to support the accustomed lifestyle and family status if it is divided. Under these terms a father chooses to create an exclusive and excluding group of himself and his favored son. It was good for the father and the favored son in the short run. The hostility created by this excusive and excluding arrangement was inevitable. That the long-range consequences were disastrous is well known.

When the Hebrew Patriarch Jacob bestowed favored status on his son Joseph, he unwittingly set up an exclusive and excluding group of himself and the chosen one. The other brothers formed another group. Joseph was a privileged insider. They were cast as outsiders; the excluded ones. They went along with this arrangement for a time, accepting it as their father's right. Yet their feelings of hostility grew until they decided to do away with their favored brother. They didn't kill him as Cain did Abel, but they did everything short of that. In both of these cases, a choice was made that seemed logical and appropriate under the circumstances. It is doubtful that any of the parties involved were aware of the principles of group dynamics and the potential disasters they were going to create with the choices they had made.

For a very long and destructive time this has been the unwitting situation with the principles of group dynamics. Without knowledge of these principles and the correlated law it has seemed just fine to form exclusive and excluding groups. They are for the good of the members. They are very often sanctioned by parents, teachers, religious leaders, and other authority figures that believe it is the right thing to do. People gain valuable benefits when they participate in them. Attacks from outsiders are puzzling and not seen as resulting from anything the members have done. Now that the principles and the correlated law have been discovered, this new information makes it imperative to change our perspective on human relations. At the same time it is now possible to avoid the disastrous consequences of exclusive and excluding behavior.

The principles of group dynamics do not call for eliminating differences and homogenizing the human race. They do not mean that people should avoid forming special groups. Quite the contrary. Besides making life interesting, diversity is absolutely essential to the ultimate survival of humankind.

Throughout human history systems of orientation and devotion have been formed around information received from the Universal Mind. The prophets who first received this information through dreams and other mystical experiences were seen to be God-like or God incarnate because of their powerful insights. The receivers and the information received became the nucleus for development of the power groups that we now call the great religions. The formation of such groups provided great comfort and support for their members. It also tended to divide and separate the peoples of the earth. The principles of group dynamics and the correlated law had not yet been revealed. The exclusive and excluding behaviors of people in these groups unwittingly resulted in terrible acts of violence in the name of religion.

There is much good to be derived from the fellowship, shared history, traditions, rituals and personal identification with any of the great religions. At the same time, there is enormous danger in regarding any group as the best and God's favorite. Everything in the universe, including the Universal Mind, has been created by the same ultimate source. This means that all of the peoples on the earth, and any peoples on any other planets or elsewhere in the universe are included. To set oneself or group apart as superior or the favorite is an exclusionary activity. It denies, it excludes, and it passes judgment. It is the problem that Cain and Abel experienced. It's the curse of Cain.

The histories of all the great religions include many terrible examples of violence and destruction related to their exclusive and excluding beliefs of superiority. In making egocentric and ethnocentric decisions without regard to the principles of group dynamics they unwittingly triggered destructive consequences for themselves and others. Is the answer to eliminate the great religions? Certainly not.

Each of the great religions has unlimited potential for creative and productive contributions to the evolution of mankind. By keeping alive the aspects of their religious orientations that provide stability and nurture the best in people. By recognizing the whole of *Homo sapiens* as a fragile and marvelous life experiment. By celebrating diversity as a blessing and the best hope for long-range survival. By finding effective ways to *exchange* important information between groups. By supporting ideas for creative and productive participation in the evolution of the human species. By embracing communication with the Universal Mind as a powerful resource for learning what we need to make our journey through the cosmos a joyful and productive ride.

There must be a concerted effort to teach all human inhabitants of the earth that diversity and unity are divinely compatible. We must get the word out. Develop practices to teach it everywhere. Everyday. Put it on bumper stickers. Develop a web site devoted to it. Use proliferating social media platforms like Face Book, Twitter, Blogs, and Google Plus to share this information with the world community. Create movies and television programs that show positive examples of it. Strive for a critical mass of earth dwellers that know and understand it. Promote all ethnic and religious affiliations as *unique teams* within the universal family of mankind that appreciate, challenge, and support each other.

People *will* exchange important information within their groups of origin and others of their choice. They need to learn how to value those affiliations *and* expand their ties with humanity at large. They need to learn the skills for participation in democratic processes. They need to learn concepts and skills for balancing autonomy and order in human relations. They need to learn about the principles and the correlated law of group dynamics. They need to learn how to see outside their own limited illusions and appreciate the illusions of others. They need to know about the great experiments in democratic governance. They need to know that the great creative and productive contributions to the betterment of mankind have come from a very wide variety of human beings, including native people often referred to as indigenous. They need to learn how to develop their abilities to communicate with the Universal Mind. They need to know that the future of the species is not set in stone. They need to know that it will be influenced by the choices people make, individually and together. Above all, their education should be focused on the fine art of choicemaking.

The eminent social theorist, Amitai Etzioni, has devoted a lifetime (with others) to the study of relationships in groups. In 1966 he published *The New Golden Rule*, a timely and powerful book that received the Simon Weisenthal Center's Tolerance Book Award. This book takes into account and builds on extensive research data and personal experience in the field. It is a "horn of plenty" for information about how to educate people about creating group relationships that celebrate diversity and foster unity.

Some of the larger corporations in the world have already discovered that healthy people in healthy organizations are more creative and productive. They are also more resilient and responsive to change, enabling the organization to make better choices for survival in dynamic marketplaces. Such organizations have brought in Organization Development (OD) consultants to help their members learn how to exchange important information, value diversity, resolve conflicts, and solve problems.

It is now clear that there can be no real peace in the world without economic justice. Although many noted injustices and violent wars have had their origins in capitalistic enterprises, capitalism, per se, is not the problem. There are positive aspects to capitalism that are of great value. It motivates. It spurs innovation. It induces commitment. It rewards creative and productive behavior. However, capitalism that is not regulated by moral imperatives and follows a course of *profits above all* violates the principles and correlated law of group dynamics. It is toxic for peace because it is exclusive and excluding. It inevitably leads to hostility. It often results in deadly conflict. Without peace the human, technological, and spiritual resources needed for making our evolutionary journey together through time and space are sinfully wasted.

* *

Gregg's thoughts suddenly shifted from the universal ideas he had learned during the span of his life to a reverie on the journey that had brought him to this place. He remembered the abuse he had suffered as a boy because he was different. Being misunderstood by folks whose illusions restricted their responses to things beyond the ordinary. Narrow escapes from real and sometimes imagined dangers. Paradoxical experiences that kept him from being programmed into a static illusion of the world. Numerous synchronistic events that expanded his awareness. Mentors who saw his potential and helped him to focus his creative energy. Timely assistance from the Universal

Mind. The continuing development of his extrasensory capabilities. His evolution from feeling like the perpetual outsider to recognition of himself as unconditionally connected. All of these things had moved him along on his extraordinary journey that transcended all of the separate steps and stages. A journey that eventually brought him to Mitchell's Point and the joyful epiphany of finding that from out there he could see forever. With expanded vision from that vantage point he was able to see many things not discernable when he was immersed in an earthbound illusion of limited scope. Out there is where he tuned in to the Universal Mind and (re)discovered a treasure of great importance to mankind: *the principles and correlated law of group dynamics.* With this information now revealed he was excited about sharing it with the world at large. He could see that this gift from the Universal Mind would enable people to celebrate their diversity while peacefully working together toward the ultimate survival of the species. Pondering the length and breadth of his life experience, he was nearly overwhelmed with feelings of deep gratitude. He was also near exhaustion and feeling the kind of bone tired that results from long and arduous travel. The siren call of his nice warm bed was whispering gently in his ears. He decided to call it a night with one more entry in his journal.

* *

Reflecting on seminal truths discovered

Every living human is on a journey. Like it or not, they are all traveling on the same vehicle; Planet Earth. And they are at a critical juncture in their journey. They are in great need of a new moral compass to guide them in making decisions about how to conduct themselves as they ride through time and space. Not to supplant religion, but to bring the best of religious thought and modern science together to formulate plans for both their current well-being and the ultimate survival of the species. They must not let a few shortsighted and greedy people capture the resources needed for this cosmic level task. *Expanded awareness, individual and together, is absolutely vital.*

The world is littered with the remains of religious systems that were built around mystical deities and attempts to lock off any further evolution of religious thought. In time, the general awareness of the public evolved to the point where these static systems were seen as incomplete and no longer supportable. Their authority to serve as moral compasses and activate moral imperatives was diminished accordingly. Only large and open systems of orientation and devotion of, by, and for the people can support the creativity and commit the resources that will be needed. Dictatorships of any kind, religious, scientific, governmental, or corporate can't make it happen because their exclusive and excluding actions shut down the free flow of information and limit access to the Universal Mind.

The issue of creationism versus evolution is an unreal dichotomy, fabricated out of fear and ignorance. They are both part of the ultimate cosmic design. The cosmos was created and the evolution of everything in it was set in motion by the same ultimate source. Change is a constant in this design. In human affairs, Darwin (at least his interpreters) and others, including Milton Friedman, Alan Greenspan, and Ayn Rand, were egregiously wrong about how positive evolutionary change is advanced. They unwittingly chose to exalt and promote obscene short-term gains for an exclusive and excluding few. Besides violating the principles of group dynamics and correlated law that would eventually cause this scheme to crash and burn, it deprived the whole human community of long-term insights and interactions vital to ultimate survival of the species. Change that is brought about by overwhelming force, shock and awe, and the power of elites tends to lock things down and promote the status quo. These approaches limit the creativity and selection from multiple elements that are the engine of evolution. On the other hand, change that stems from realizing and promoting a positive new cultural story or myth, such as the move from polytheistic to monotheistic religious systems three thousand years ago, gains voluntary commitment that advances the cause of evolution. At least until fear and greed cause misguided folks to put a fence around a part of it and try to control that much for their own benefit. The current conditions of great chaos and stress in our world offer myriad wonderful opportunities to creatively aid the evolutionary process. We can help make the world a better place for the positive development for all of human life. It depends on what we do with these opportunities.

With a little help, the unwitting passengers riding on the earth *can* learn to see where they are in the cosmos. They can view the death of their sun and solar system from Mitchell's Point. They can learn to see this inevitable event as presenting a cosmic opportunity rather than a tragic end. They can establish the readiness to live elsewhere or in some other way as a *superordinate goal.* Such a goal can stimulate successive generations to communicate more fully with the Universal Mind and develop the qualities they will need for their part of the job. They can realize that the cosmic journey of *Homo sapiens* is infinitely larger than individual lifetimes. They can become aware that some of what lives within humans during a single life span can continue the journey within their descendents, ad infinitum. With an evolving moral compass and moral imperatives created by religion and science working together, they can stay focused on their roles as stewards of the life units entrusted to them. Energized and guided by that perspective they can reverently care for their home base (space ship earth) while at the same time developing the technology to take its passengers safely to new galactic homes.

Our collective awareness has evolved from having no idea how our planet looked, to having beautiful blue-white images photographed by astronauts widely available and firmly fixed in our minds. We now know that our eighty trips around the sun are not actually a series of completed circles. Because the sun is also constantly moving along its own trajectory, a computer model of our annual cycles around it, and simultaneously through space, would be configured as a spiral. A digital picture of the path of our circumnavigations would look a lot like an enormous corkscrew. Besides being a fascinating figure to behold, a spiral is open. It transcends the closure associated with going round and round in tight repetitive circles.

As we spiral through space, riding on our fragile earth ship, there is a special resource we can call upon to help us make a safe and rewarding journey. The ancients conceived of the *Phoenix* as a reminder to us that we have the power to re-create ourselves when it becomes clear that the *old* is not working anymore. Phoenix energy can give us the opportunity to put an end to the old way of doing things, and the old way of regarding ourselves. It can enable us to enter into a new place where we can create ourselves as fresh and dynamic new persons. Working together, we can use our Phoenix energy to exponentially increase our power to perceive and create. With help from the Universal Mind, we can invent new ways to care for the marvelous planet that serves as both our home and our means of transport into the future. As our evolutionary journey through time and space unfolds, we can *ride with the Phoenix* out to Mitchell's Point and other cosmic vistas where we can discover more of what it will take for safe and creative navigation.

Insightful earth dwellers are rapidly becoming aware that the cosmos and life within it operates in *cycles* at every level. They are leading the way to greater understanding and better choice making in view of that awareness. As we learn more about how the universal cycles are manifested in our lives, it will bring us great opportunities. These can serve as guide maps to help us find our way to the great cyclical junctures (tipping points) where our choice making can have the most power to serve the common good. As we learn more about how to communicate with the Universal Mind, it appears that even the direction of our evolution can be influenced by our thoughts and the choices we make. By choosing to bring the best of science and religion together as working partners, we may have a shot at learning to work in harmony with the cycles that affect us. We have learned that our own galaxy is one among millions. We have come to understand that all of us earth travelers constitute but one strand in a complex web of life. Slowly and surely, we are collectively ushering in a new golden age made possible by riding with the phoenix into an era of cosmic awareness. Where that takes us, and how it affects us, will depend on the choices we make, individually and together.

SELECTED BIBLIOGRAPHY

Atwater, P.M.H. *Beyond The Light: What Isn't Being Said About Near-Death Experience.* Seacaucus, N.J.: Birch Lane Press Books of Carol Publishing Group, 1994.

Bacevich, Andrew J. *The Limits of Power: The End of American Exceptionalism.* New York: Metropolitan Books, A Division of Henry Holt and Company LLC. 2008.

Batra, Ravi. *The New Golden Age: The Coming Revolution Against Political Corruption And Economic Chaos.* New York: Palgrave Macmillan, 2007.

Bourne, Edmund J., PH.D. *Global Shift: How a New Worldview Is Transforming Humanity.* Oakland, CA: New Harbinger Productions, Inc., 2008.

Brinkley, Dannion with Paul Perry. *Saved By The Light: The True Story of a Man Who Died Twice and the Profound Revelations He Received.* New York: Villard Books of Random House, Inc., 1994.

Bucke, Richard Maurice, M.D. *Cosmic Consciousness: A Study in the Evolution of the Human Mind.* Bedford, Massachusetts: Applewood Books Classic Reprint, 2000.

Carroll, Lee and Jan Tober. *The Indigo Children: The New Kids Have Arrived.* Carlsbad, California: Hay House, Inc., 1999.

Cerminara, Gina. *The World Within.* Virginia Beach, Virginia: A.R.E. Press, 1985.

Dewey, John. *Democracy and Education: An Introduction to the Philosophy of Education. New York: The MacMillan Company, 1916.*

_____. *Experience & Education.* New York: Collier Books of The Macmillan Company, First Printing 1963, Sixth Printing 1966.

Dossey, Larry, M.D. *Healing Words: The Power of Prayer and* the *Practice of Medicine.* New York: Harper Collins Publishers, 1993.

_____. *Be Careful What You Pray For: You Just Might Get It.* New York: Harper Collins Publishers, 1998.

_____. *Reinventing Medicine: Beyond Mind-Body to a New Era of Healing.* San Francisco: Harper San Francisco of Harper Collins Publishers, 1999.

Eisler, Riane. *The Real Wealth of Nations: Creating A Caring Economics.* San Francisco: Berrett-Koehler Publishers, Inc. A BK Currents Book. 2007.

Etzioni, Amitai. *The New Golden Rule: Community and Morality in a Democratic Society.* New York: Basic Books of Perseus Books Group, 1996.

Friedman, Norman. *Bridging Science and Spirit: Common Elements in David Bohm's Physics.* The Perennial Philosophy and Seth. St. Louis, Missouri: Living Lake Books, 1994.

Fromm, Erich. The Sane Society. New York: Rinehart Publishers, *1955.*

_____. *The Art of Loving. New York:* Harper and Row Publishers, 1956, 1989.

Gerber, Richard, M.D. *Vibrational Medicine: New Choices for Healing Ourselves.* Santa Fe, New Mexico: Bear & Company Publishers, 1988.

Gleick, James. *CHAOS: Making a New Science.* New York: Penguin Books of Viking Penguin, Inc., 1987.

Harman, Willis. *Global Mind Change: The Promise of the 21ˢ'Century (second edition).* San Francisco: Berrett-Koehler Publishers, Inc. and The Institute of Noetic Sciences, 1998.

Hawkins, David R., M.D., Ph.D., *Power Versus Force: The Hidden Determinants of Human Behavior.* Carlsbad, California: Hay House, Inc. 2008.

Hoffer, Eric. *The True Believer: Thoughts on the Nature of Mass Movements.* New York: Harper and Row Publishers, Inc., 1951, 1966, 1989.

Homans, George C. *The Human Group.* London: Routledge & K. Paul Ltd., Original Publication 1951; New Brunswick, N.J.: Transaction Publishers, 1992, 1995

Hopke, Robert H. *There Are No Accidents: Synchronicity and the Stories of Our Lives.* New York: Riverhead Books of the Berkeley Publishing Group, 1997.

Houston, Jean (with Margaret Rubin). *Manual for the Peacemaker: An Iroquois Legend to Heal Self & Society.* Wheaton, Illinois: Quest Books of The Theosophical Publishing House, 1995.

Houston, Jean. *The Wizard Of Us: Transformational Lessons from Oz.* New York: Atria Books, A Division of Simon and Schuster, Inc., 2012.

Hunt, Valerie V. *Infinite Mind: The Science of Human Vibrations.* Malibu, California: Malibu Publishing Company, 1995.

Katra, Jane, Ph.D. and Targ, Russell. *The Heart of the Mind: How to Experience God Without Belief* Novato, California: New World Library, 1999.

Klein, Naomi. *The Shock Doctrine: The Rise of Disaster Capitalism.* New York: Metropolitan Books, A Division of Henry Holt and Company, LLC, 2007.

_____. *How To Build A New World: Why I was Wrong in the Shock Doctrine and What We Must Do Now.* New York: The Progressive Magazine, Volume 77, Number 12/01, December/January Issue, Pages 42-45, 2013.

Loukatos, Panagiotes (translated by Mark Frangiadakis). *Delphi: Legends and History.* Athens, Greece: George Papademetriou Publisher, 1962.

Mandela, Nelson. *Notes To The Future: Words of Wisdom.* New York: Atria Books, A Division of Simon and Schuster, Inc., 2012.

Mankiller, Wilma (with Michael Wallis). A Chief and Her People: *An Autobiography by the Principal Chief of the Cherokee Nation.* New York: St. Martin's Press, 1993.

Miller, Alice (translated by Ruth Ward). *The Drama Of The Gifted Child: The Search for the True Self.* New York: Basic Books of Harper Collins Publishers, 1994.

Mayer, Elizabeth Lloyd, PH.D. *Extraordinary Knowing: Science, Skepticism, and the Inexplicable Powers Of The Human Mind.* New York: Bantam Dell, A Division of Random House, Inc., 2007.

McTaggart, Lynne. *The Intention Experiment: Using Your Thoughts to Change Your Life and the World.* New York: Free Press, A Division of Simon and Schuster, Inc. 2007.

_____. *The Field (updated edition): The Quest For The secret Force of the Universe.* New York: Harper Collins Publishers. 2008.

Miller, Alice (translated by Ruth Ward). *The Drama Of The Gifted Child: The Search for the True Self.* New York: Basic Books of Harper Collins Publishers, 1994.

Miller, Henry. *The Colussus of Marussi.* New York: New Directions Publishing Corporation, 1941.

Millman, Dan. *The Life You Were Born To Live: A Guide to* Finding *Your Life Purpose.* Tiburon, California: H J Kramer Inc, 1993.

Mitchell, Dr. Edgar D. (with Dwight Williams). *The Way of The Explorer: An Apollo Astronaut's Journey Through the* Material *and Mystical Worlds.* New York: G. P. Putnam's Sons, 1996.

Monroe, Robert A. *Journeys Out of the Body.* Main Street Books of Bantam Doubleday Dell Publishing Group, Inc., 1977.

Morse, Melvin, M.D. with Paul Perry. *Closer to the Light: Learning From the Near-Death Experiences of Children.* New York: Ivy Books of Ballantine Books, 1990.

_____*Parting Visions: Uses and Meanings of Pre-Death, Psychic, and Spiritual*

Experiences. New York: Harper Paperbacks of Harper Collins Publishers, 1994.

O'Murchu, Diarmuid. M.S.C., *Quantum Theology: Spiritual Implications Of The New Physics.* New York: The Crossword Publishing Company, 1998.

Mullen, William. *Dinosaur Bones in Sahara Prove a Monster Find.* Chicago: Chicago Tribune, November 12, 1999, Section 1, Pages 1 and 28.

Muller, Wayne. *Legacy of the Heart: The Spiritual Advantages of a Painful Childhood.* New York: A Fireside Book Published by Simon & Schuster, 1992.

Myss, Caroline, Ph.D. *Anatomy of the Spirit: The Seven Stages of Power and Healing.* New York: Three Rivers Press of Crown Publishers, Inc., 1996.

Ornstein, Robert, PH.D. *The Evolution Of Consciousness.* New York: Prentice Hall Press, 1991.

Parker, Alice Anne. *Understand Your Dreams: 1500 Basic Dream Images and How to Interpret Them.* Tiburon, California: H J Kramer, Inc., 1995.

Radin, Dean, Ph.D. *The Conscious Universe: The Scientific Truth of Psychic Phenomena.* New York: Harperedge Division of Harpercollins Publishers, Inc., 1997.

_____. *Entangled Minds: Extrasensory Experiences In A Quantum Reality.* New York: Pocket Books, A Division of Simon & Schuster, Inc., 2006.

Redfield, James. *The Tenth Insight: Holding The Vision.* New York: Warner Books, Inc., 1996.

_____. *The Celestine Vision: Living The New Spiritual Awareness.* New York: Warner Books, Inc., 1997.

Rossi, Ernest Lawrence, Ph.D. *The Psychobiology of Mind-Body Healing: New Concepts of Therapeutic Hypnosis.* New York: W.W. Norton& Company, Inc. 1986.

_____. *Symptom Path To Enlightenment: The New Dynamics of Self-Organization in Psychotherapy.*

Pacific Palisades, California: Palisades Gateway Publishing Company, 1996.

Scharmer, Otto and Kaufer, Katrin. *Leading From The Emerging Future: From Ego-System to Eco-System Economies. San Francisco: Berrett-KoehlerPublisher, Inc. A BK Currents Book, 2013.*

Schnabel, Jim. *Remote Viewers: The Secret History of America's Psychic Spies.* Dell Books of Bantam Doubleday Dell Publishing Group, Inc., 1997.

Schwartz, Regina M. *The Curse of Cain: The Violent Legacy of Monotheism.* Chicago: The University of Chicago Press, 1997.

Stanford, Gene. *Developing Effective Classroom Groups: A Practical Guide For Teachers.* New York: Hart Publishing Company, Inc., 1977.

Sparks, John B. Histomap of Religion: Man's Search for Spiritual Unity. Chicago: Rand McNally Company, 1966.

Serena, Melody with Photographs by David Doubilet. *Duck-Billed Platypus: Australia's Urban Oddity.* National Geographic, April 2000, Pages 118 - 129.

Sugrue, Thomas. *There is a River: The Story of Edgar Cayce. (revised edition)* Virginia Beach, Virginia: A.R.E. Press, 1994.

Targ, Russell and Jane Katra, Ph.D. *Miracles of Mind: Exploring Nonlocal Consciousness and Spiritual Healing.* Novato, California: New World Library, 1998.

Targ, Russell. *Limitless Mind: A Guide to Remote Viewing and Transformation of Consciousness.* Novato, California: New World Library. 2004.

_____. *The Reality Of ESP: A Physicist's Proof Of Psychic Abilities.* Wheaton, Illinois: Quest Books, 2012.

Thurston, Mark, Ph.D. *Millenium Prophecies: Predictions for* the *Coming Century from Edgar Cayce.* New York: Barnes & Noble Books, 1999.

Vandenberg, Phillip (translated by George Unwin). *The Mysteries of the Oracles: The Last Secrets of Antiquity.* New York: Macmillan Publishing Company, Inc., 2007.

Walsh, Neal Donald. *Conversations With God: An Uncommon Dialogue (book 1).* New York: G. P. Putnam's Sons, 1996.

_____. *Conversations With God: An Uncommon Dialogue (book 2).* Charlottesville, Virginia: Hampton Roads Publishing Company, Inc., 1997.

Wilber, Ken. *Integral Spirituality: A Startling New Role for Religion in the Modern and Postmodern World.* Boston: Integral Books, 2006.

Wilkins, Sir Hubert and Sherman, Harold M. *Thoughts Through Space: A Remarkable Adventure in the Realm of Mind.* Charlottsville, Virginia: Hampton Roads Publishing Company, Inc., 2004.

Zeig, Jeffrey K., Ph.D. *Experiencing Erickson: An Introduction to the Man and his Work.* New York: Brunner/Mazel, Inc., 1985.

ABOUT THE AUTHOR

George E. Monroe grew up in a small town in the southern hill country of America's heartland where his creative learning style was not always understood or appreciated. His *different* insights were often challenged or rejected by his family and others in the provincial environs of his home community. At the same time, numerous experiences of guided serendipity, including the timely appearances of caring mentors, enabled him to transcend these limitations and become a gifted teacher. In subject areas ranging from social studies to science, and at grade levels from elementary to graduate school, he has always vigorously pursued cutting edge information to help himself and his students *think outside the box.*

He obtained his Ph.D. in an interdisciplinary program focused on facilitating change processes in educational organizations. Completion of post-doctoral programs also enabled him to become a Licensed Clinical Psychologist and an Approved Consultant in Clinical Hypnosis.

After fourteen years of teaching and developing outreach programs at the University of Illinois in Chicago, he left academia to establish a private practice of psychotherapy and clinical hypnosis.

He currently serves as Vice Chairman of the Board of Directors of the Fund For The Erevna International Peace (FEIPC), a non-profit organization incorporated in the State of Maryland, USA, that supports development of he Erevna International Peace Center (EIPC) headquartered on the Island of Cyprus.

The EIPC has been granted Roster Consultative Status with the Economic and Social Council (ECOSOC) of the United Nations and he is a designated Representative of the EIPC for participation in ECOSOC functions and programs at the UN Headquarters in New York. For details on the FEIPC and its relationship to the EIPC, see the website, www.feipc.org.

Dr. Monroe currently resides with his wife, Merle, in Evanston, Illinois.